Oedipus Rex

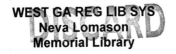

Publication of this volume has been made possible in part

through the generous support and enduring vision of

Warren G. Moon.

Oedipus Rex

SOPHOCLES

A verse translation by

David Mulroy,

with introduction and notes

The University of Wisconsin Press

The University of Wisconsin Press
1930 Monroe Street, 3rd Floor
Madison, Wisconsin 53711-2059
uwpress.wisc.edu

3 Henrietta Street
London WC2E 8LU, England
eurospanbookstore.com

1   3   5   4   2

Printed in the United States of America

Library of Congress Cataloging-in-Publication Data
Sophocles.
[Oedipus Rex. English]
Oedipus Rex / Sophocles; a verse translation by David Mulroy,
with introduction and notes.
p.   cm. — (Wisconsin studies in classics)
ISBN 978-0-299-28254-7 (pbk.: alk. paper)
ISBN 978-0-299-28253-0 (e-book)
1. Oedipus (Greek mythology) — Drama.
I. Mulroy, David D., 1943–   II. Title.
III. Series: Wisconsin studies in classics.
PA4414.O7M75   2011
882′.01—dc22   2010041229

To

Marc Boucher

and

Rick Krause

Contents

Preface

The Goals of This Translation

Many fine translations of *Oedipus Rex* have been published in recent years. Why another?

This volume was designed to answer a need that I have felt in teaching Greek tragedy in translation. In my experience, available translations fail to convey the essential fact that Greek tragedies as originally performed were—in one word—dynamic. The convention of translating choral odes into free verse with its characteristic obscurity is partially responsible for this failure. The general reader of such translations is perplexed by the cryptic reflections of "Strophe" and "Antistrophe," whose main purpose seems to be to delay the action. For the original audiences, on the other hand, the songs of the chorus were the best-loved parts of most tragedies. Among the anecdotes reflecting their popular appeal is the story that Athenian prisoners of war in Sicily were able to buy their freedom by teaching their captors choral songs by Euripides (Plutarch, *Life of Nicias* 29.3).

One of the goals of my translation is to convey the fact that strophes and antistrophes were stanzas of easily learned songs, sung and danced to by a chorus. These musical interludes represented the release of pent-up tension, an explosion of energy. As in all good songs, the basic sentiments were readily accessible, and the sounds of the words were as important as their meanings. What made the sound of the words memorable was the fact that they fit perfectly with the melody to which they were set. This is reflected in the fact that successive stanzas, strophes and antistrophes, are metrically identical. In addition, normal idiom was distorted to create echoes between strophes and antistrophes. Such wordplay, together with the observance of a rigid metrical pattern, created a substratum of purely aesthetic pleasure that tempered the high seriousness of the sentiments expressed and facilitated memorization.

To reproduce something of that effect, I have translated the choral odes into short rhymed stanzas. Of course, this strategy leaves me open to criticism on two fronts: the Greeks did not use end rhyme, and the meters of their choral odes were more complicated than the ones I use here. On the other hand, some compromise is inevitable in translating. It's my belief that short, rhymed, songlike stanzas are for modern English-speaking readers the practical equivalent of the odes of Greek tragedy.

The spoken parts of a Greek tragedy pose a similar challenge. For a person reading Sophocles' *Oedipus Rex* in Greek, the first few lines establish a rhythm that is sustained throughout the spoken portions of the play. The rhythm is created by the arrangement of "long" and "short" syllables. The former are those containing a prolonged vowel sound or ending in two or more consonants. Other syllables are short. Long and short syllables are arranged into "iambic trimeters," three pairs of disyllabic poetic feet. In each pair, the first foot may be an iamb (short-long) or a spondee (long-long) while the second must be an iamb. In other words, the syllables fit into this pattern of necessarily long (–), necessarily short (˘), and either long or short (x) syllables:

$$x - \smile - / x - \smile - / x - \smile -$$

Occasionally, a long syllable is resolved into two short ones. Otherwise, Sophocles' speeches adhere rigidly to this pattern. It is not known exactly how these iambic trimeters were originally supposed to sound, but in one way or another, the necessarily long syllables were especially prominent. However the Greek is read, their regular occurrence creates a perceptible rhythm. The Greek text has a constant forward momentum. Nothing precludes changes in tempo, but there is no room for long silences or inarticulate cries or groans—a fact reflected in the ancient biography of Sophocles. According to one version of his death, the aged poet was reading *Antigone* aloud and near the end came to a long passage with no pauses. Straining to complete it, he ran out of breath and died![1] Of course, the story is apocryphal, but it reflects the expectation that speeches in tragedy would maintain forward momentum. Moreover, because of the natural tendency to assimilate grammatical structures to metrical units, clauses and sentences tended to be short and to the point. That tendency comes to the surface in passages called *stichomythia* ("line-speech"), in which characters exchange remarks that take up exactly one or two trimeters apiece. Compared with epic poetry, the spoken parts of Greek tragedy are downright telegraphic, a point made by Aristotle, who calls iambic verse "kinetic" (*Poetics* 1459b33–35).

Available translations do not seem to me to capture this conciseness or forward momentum. Prose and free-verse translations have other goals entirely. Attempts like mine to translate the spoken parts on a line-by-line basis into English blank verse lead almost inevitably to the use of iambic pentameter. Not only do English-speaking readers expect pentameters, but English is more economical in its use of syllables than an inflected language like Greek. Hence, the thought expressed by twelve Greek syllables often lends itself to a ten-syllable English translation. There are, of course, good translations of *Oedipus Rex* that use pentameters, but in my view they are somewhat too free metrically, admitting enough irregularities to obscure the regular rhythm and derail the momentum.

In this work I have used fairly strict iambic pentameters. My only intentional irregularities consist of trochees instead of iambs in the first foot and spondees at any point in the line. Every line also contains a caesura, a break or momentary pause created by the occurrence of a word ending in a trochee instead of an iamb. That seems to me to be essential to the creation of rhythmic lines. Even though they technically fit the pattern, English pentameters that consist entirely of monosyllables or iambic words or both do not sound genuinely rhythmic to me.

Otherwise, I have tried to do full justice to the literal meaning of Sophocles' words and to the quality of his diction, which is elevated but not overwrought. In translating the choral odes into rhymed stanzas, I could not adhere to the traditional line divisions. Hence I have just indicated the lines at which each unit, strophe or antistrophe, begins and ends.

Spelling Proper Names

The spelling of ancient Greek proper names poses a problem. When Greek literature was translated, discussed, and adapted by later Latin-writing authors, proper names were Latinized. Some Greek phonemes were changed to their nearest regularly occurring Latin counterparts instead of being transliterated letter for letter. Thus Greek *Oidipous* became *Oedipus*. These Latinized names were in turn adopted by English writers and given English pronunciations and accents, so that English dictionaries include *Oedipus* (ē´-də-pəs), not *Oidipous* (oi-dee´-poos), and *Jocasta* (jō-kas´-tə) instead of *Iokaste* (ē-ō-kas´-tā). In recent years, more and more translators and scholars have used original Greek spellings in the interest of greater authenticity. I've resisted this trend, using the Latinized (or Anglicized) versions of proper names for ease of pronunciation by English-speaking readers. In one way at least, the effect achieved is closer to the experience of the original Greek audience, since the proper names in the play did not sound like elements of a foreign language to them.

Introduction and Footnotes

In writing my Introduction I had general readers, nonspecialists, in mind. More specifically, I was thinking of the great friends with whom I occasionally meet for "great books" roundtable discussions. I have tried to provide the kind of peripheral information that facilitates discussion of the text itself and prevents tangents based on false assumptions about its context. Hence I provide a thumbnail history of Greece and a summary of some of the issues that have arisen in the secondary literature, such as the question of whether Oedipus has a "tragic flaw." One appendix offers a synopsis of Sophocles' entire Theban trilogy, since "What happened next?" is bound to come up in discussions of *Oedipus Rex*; another appendix spells out the riddle of the Sphinx, which Sophocles himself never did. A bibliography points to further readings on these and other subjects.

My footnotes were written with the same general readers in mind. I have tried to be alert to the points in the play where such readers are likely to ask themselves, "Now, what is *that* supposed to mean?" and to provide complete but concise answers. I also use the footnotes to indicate problems in the text: that is, passages where there is significant disagreement among experts about what Sophocles actually wrote or what he meant by what he wrote.

Both in the Introduction and in the footnotes, I have refrained from imposing my own interpretation on the play. Given a certain amount of basic information, the general reader is well qualified to interpret a work dealing with such universal themes. If the play seems to mean different things to different people, this is not the result of incompetence on the part of some. Certain details of Oedipus' life and character were left indeterminate by Sophocles. It is natural for readers to fill in those aspects on the basis of their own experiences and feelings. Hence the Oedipus that any reader sees is partially a reflection, as unique as the reader himself or herself.

Texts

In doing this translation, I have relied primarily on the following texts and commentaries: R. C. Jebb, *Sophocles: Plays: Oedipus Tyrannus* (Cambridge University Press, 1893), reprinted with introduction by J. Rusten (Bristol Classical Press, 2004); R. D. Dawe (ed.), *Sophocles, Oedipus Rex* (rev. ed., Cambridge University Press, 1982); Jean Bollack, *L'Oedipe roi de Sophocle: Le texte et ses interpretations* (Presses Universitaires de Lille, 1990); H. L. Jones and N. G. Wilson, *Sophoclis Fabulae* (Oxford University Press, 1990); and H. L. Jones, *Sophocles: Ajax, Electra, Oedipus Tyrannus*, Loeb Classical Library (Harvard University Press, 1994).

Notes

1. S. Radt, *Tragicorum Graecorum Fragmenta* (Göttingen: Vandenhoeck and Ruprecht, 1977), 4:36–37. Translated in M. Lefkowitz, *The Lives of the Greek Poets* (Baltimore, MD: Johns Hopkins University Press, 1981), 160–63.

Introduction

Historical Background

The Age of Mycenae (1600–1200 BCE): The Historical Setting of Greek Myths and Legends

Greek myths and legends, such as those concerning Oedipus, were passed along orally by imaginative storytellers for hundreds of years before they were written down. Hence they are mostly fictional. They do, however, have an authentic historical setting: the Mycenaean Period, when Greek-speaking people made their first appearance in world history. Archaeology shows that they had settled in Greece by 1600 BCE. The first settlement from this period to be excavated was at Mycenae in southern Greece, whose impressive remains lent credence to the legend that Agamemnon, a king of Mycenae, was the leader of the Greek armies during the Trojan War. Evidence of major settlements dated to this period turned up in Athens, Iolcus, which is associated with the legend of Jason and the Argonauts, and Thebes, Oedipus' hometown. Heracles, the son of Zeus and greatest of all heroes, had a Mycenaean mother, but he grew up in Thebes.

The prosperity of Mycenaean Greece was short-lived. Archaeology shows that starting around 1200 BCE, the major settlements were destroyed and abandoned. Only Athens seems to have escaped. It is not known what led to all this destruction. Perhaps an economic collapse led to a period of chaos and pillaging. Whatever the disruption was, its effects extended beyond the Mycenaean world. Hattusas, the capital city of the Hittites, was burnt to the ground, and the Egyptian pharaoh Rameses III boasts of his destruction of a marauding horde, the "peoples of the sea," who invaded his land with the worst of intentions. The city of Troy, located on the shore of present-day Turkey, just south of the mouth of the Hellespont, also seems to have been destroyed by warfare during this period. The legendary Trojan War was just one chapter in a long story of violence and destruction.

The Dark Age (1200–800 BCE): The Growth of the Oral Tradition

The collapse of Mycenae was followed by what is called the Dark Age, although archaeologists and historians who specialize in the period dislike the term, which conjures up a picture of utter desolation that is undoubtedly misleading. There is evidence that foreign trade continued, and the Greeks established some foreign colonies at this time. Nevertheless, very few luxury items from this period have been found. The palaces were gone, and they had not yet been replaced by walled cities. The population decreased, and there is no evidence of literacy. The age was at least somewhat dim.

There was one undeniable bright spot. The Dark Age Greeks developed a rich oral tradition inspired by memories of the wealth and power of their Mycenaean ancestors. The tradition was embodied primarily in the songs of bards, who traveled from settlement to settlement singing in return for food and gifts.

Many of their stories were inspired by the Greeks' religious observances. Each locale had favorite gods and goddesses to whom its inhabitants prayed and offered sacrifice. The oral tradition sifted out the most important stories and wove them together into a coherent picture, which achieved its definitive form in the poems of Homer and Hesiod. There the most important gods are imagined as a large, dysfunctional family living on Mount Olympus and answering to Zeus, the supreme authority, and Hera, his wife and sister.

Down on earth, the cities of Mycenae and Thebes come to the fore as the great capitals of the heroic world of memory. Thebes in central Greece is founded by Cadmus, an exiled Phoenician prince; Mycenae in the south by Zeus's son, Perseus. Although he does not know it at first, Oedipus is the fifth descendant of Cadmus to rule Thebes. When he abdicates because of the misfortunes dramatized in *Oedipus Rex*, his sons, Polynices and Eteocles, fight over the throne. The strife unleashed by their struggles leads to the destruction of Thebes by Mycenae and its allies a generation later. Thereafter Mycenae, now ruled by Agamemnon, becomes the dominant power in Greece and takes charge of the great expedition against Troy. The best-known legends of Greece conclude with the story of that war and the travails of its heroes, especially Odysseus, when they finally turn toward home. Whatever its nature, the cataclysm that caused the actual destruction of the Mycenaean settlements in 1200 BCE is not represented in myth and legend.

The Archaic Age (800–500 BCE): Enter the Polis

Greece began growing more populous and prosperous in the eleventh century (1100–1000 BCE). By the middle of the eighth century, these changes had added up to a complete transformation. The Greeks increasingly came together in well-organized communities, city-states or *poleis* (singular *polis*). The polis typically included a walled city with a public space or agora and shrines and temples. The poleis were governed by codes of law that gave free adult male citizens fundamentally equal rights. Residents of the surrounding countryside were also considered citizens of the polis, their inclusion symbolized by temples and shrines built in outlying areas.

Increasing population led to land shortages in many poleis. The problem was solved by the establishment of colonies, new poleis, that quickly spread across the Mediterranean wherever there were fertile fields, good harbors, and an absence of powerful rivals. The colonies were inhabited by citizens of their mother cities who had been encouraged and sometimes forced to leave their homes. One inducement to settle in a foreign colony was that each of the settlers received an equal parcel of land in his new home; in the old country, poleis were dominated by noble families who owned the best real estate and dominated political offices. Sometimes the power of such families was broken by a popular leader or "tyrant" who gained control of a polis by force and ran it ostensibly on behalf of the people as a whole. Tyrants, however, were inclined to abuse their power. Athenian democracy originated as a middle course between oppression by noble families and autocratic tyrants.

The Origin of Greek Tragedy in the Late Archaic Age

The sudden dynamism of Greek culture epitomized by the proliferation of prosperous poleis in the eighth century has never been fully explained. One contributing factor was the invention of the Greek alphabet, which also occurred around 800. One of its first uses was to record the poems that had taken shape in oral tradition, especially those attributed to Homer and Hesiod.

Those poems were the most influential ones that took shape during the Archaic Age, but they were by no means the only ones. Archilochus, Sappho, and other famous poets composed short personal poems; others turned to long, elaborate songs performed by choruses. Some choral songs were called "dithyrambs." No early examples of these survive, but they are said to have been energetic songs recounting the deeds of Dionysus, the god of wine and revelry. Their narratives were broken down into exchanges between a chorus singing in unison and the leader of the chorus, who sang or spoke as an individual. According to Aristotle (*Poetics* 1449a10), Greek tragedy evolved out of dithyrambs. First one, then two, and finally three speaking actors were introduced to enact the story narrated by the chorus and its leader. If at first dithyrambs focused on Dionysus, they soon branched out to deal with the whole range of myth and legend.

Near the end of the Archaic Age, Athens began its ascent to a position of cultural leadership in the Greek world. This was due in part to the efforts of the tyrant Pisistratus and his sons, who controlled Athens from about 561 to 510 BCE. Good rulers generally, they did much to beautify the city and patronize the arts. Among other things, they are credited with the establishment of the City Dionysia, a yearly festival in honor of Dionysus held in late March or early April. At the heart of the original festival were competitions for dithyrambic choruses. At some point in the late sixth century, tragedies evolved as a distinctive type of performance and were added to the Dionysia's events. Tragedies were presented at other festivals in Athens and in other poleis, but productions at the City Dionysia were the most prestigious, setting the standard for others. Although the stories dramatized were theoretically set in the Mycenaean Age, the way of life that they depicted bore an unmistakable resemblance to that of a Greek polis. Greek tragedy evolved into something like a mirror in which the polis, especially Athens, examined itself critically.

The Classical Age (500–300 BCE): The Rise of Athens

Events around the turn of the fifth century BCE transformed Athens into a world power and inaugurated the Classical Age. Though Pisistratus' tyranny had been benign, his eldest son, Hippias, became harsh and oppressive when his brother was murdered in a private dispute. The Athenian nobles managed to dislodge him and his family with the help of Athens' great rival, the city-state Sparta. A period of political unrest ensued. The upshot was a revision of Athenian laws that represents the beginning of Athenian democracy. Henceforth the citizens' assembly was the highest authority.

At this time too, Greek poleis on the coast of modern Turkey had come into conflict with powers to the east. By 500 they had been subjugated by the Persians, who then controlled the entire Near East, from the Persian Gulf to Egypt. In 494 the Athenians assisted an abortive attempt by the eastern poleis to liberate themselves from the Persians. The rebels were quickly crushed, and to punish the Athenians for helping them, the Persian emperor Darius dispatched an army against Athens in 490. Although outnumbered, the Athenian army stood up to the Persians on the beach of Marathon, charging them on the run and driving them back into the sea.

Ten years later the Persians returned, seeking revenge. They were led by Darius' son, King Xerxes, in person. The size of his forces was greatly exaggerated by the historian of record, Herodotus, who writes of millions of Persian soldiers. In fact, there were probably something on the order of fifty thousand soldiers and a couple hundred ships. In any event, their hopes were dashed in a series of famous battles: Thermopylae,

Artemisium, Salamis, Plataea. From Marathon on, Greek superiority in equipment, tactics, and morale was decisive.

Sophocles' Youth, His Early Career, and the Festival of Dionysus

Sophocles was born about 495 BCE. He was thus a young child in Athens during the battle of Marathon and a teenager when the enemy was defeated at Salamis. For most of the details of his life, our only source is an ancient anonymous biography, which, like others of its time, is far from reliable. Some of its statements are based on the assumption that events in Sophocles' tragedies reflected his life; others, on caricatures of him found in comedies. With that caveat, his birthplace is said to have been Colonus, a suburb of Athens (and the setting of his last play, *Oedipus at Colonus*). He is thought to have held at least two high political offices, serving a term as, in effect, the secretary of the treasury and then as a general in a war between Athens and the island state of Samos. These honors would make it likely that he was a member of the Athenian nobility and well-to-do by birth, although nothing is known for sure about his parents. His ancient biography paints him as charming, universally popular, and blessed with great musical talent. It says he was chosen at age sixteen to lead the chorus of boys who sang and danced at Athens' celebration of its victory at Salamis.

As Sophocles was growing up, the City Dionysia was also achieving its final form. After two days devoted to a ceremonial procession and other preliminaries, competition began with dithyrambic choruses. Each of ten artificial "tribes" into which the democratic constitution divided the citizens was represented by one chorus of fifty boys and one of fifty men. Then came the tragedies. On each of the next three days, one of the three poets selected by a magistrate on the merits of his scripts presented a tetralogy, a set of four plays: three tragedies and a light-hearted parody or "satyr play." On the fifth and final day, five comic dramatists competed with one play each. At the end of each set of performances, a panel of judges—spectators selected at random, one from each of the ten tribes—voted for their favorites.

Tragedies were performed by choruses that originally had twelve and later fifteen members and three speaking actors. The speaking actors wore masks and were thus able to play multiple parts. In *Oedipus Rex*, for example, the first actor plays Oedipus; the second, Creon, Tiresias, and the messenger from Corinth; and the third, the priest of Zeus, Jocasta, Laius' man, and the messenger from inside the palace.

Plays were originally performed in an orchestra or dancing area in the Athenian agora. In the course of the fifth century, they were moved to the Theater of Dionysus, an outdoor amphitheater on the southern slope of the Acropolis. It was not originally an elaborate edifice. In Sophocles' day, most of the spectators sat on wooden benches or bare ground. There was a terraced dancing area and beyond that a wooden stage building where actors changed costumes and from which they entered the action on stage. The wall of the stage building that faced the audience provided a backdrop. It is not known for sure whether the actors stood on a raised stage or were on the same plane as the chorus. Plays began with prologues in which the dramatic situation was revealed through the remarks of one or more of the actors. That was followed by the entrance of the chorus, singing an ode that identified them and explained their presence. During the rest of the play, spoken passages dominated by actors alternated with choral songs and dances, but the separation was not absolute. Actors sometimes broke into song, while the leader of the chorus regularly engaged in spoken exchanges with the actors.

It seems that Sophocles first competed as playwright in the City Dionysia of 469 or 468. Since only three tragedians were chosen to compete, this was an honor in itself. One of his competitors that year was Aeschylus, the leading dramatist of the day. Nevertheless, Sophocles won first place with *Triptolemus* (now lost, along with the rest of that year's entries), a play about the young hero from nearby Eleusis, the site of a great temple of Demeter, goddess of grain. The mythical Triptolemus spread knowledge of the cultivation of grain to the whole world, flying from place to place in a chariot pulled by winged serpents.

Early in his career, Sophocles acted and sang in the plays that he wrote. What we hear about these performances suggests that his early works lacked the high seriousness of his later ones. He is said to have charmed audiences with his impersonation of Nausicaa, the princess in the *Odyssey* who helped the desperate, naked Odysseus obtain the hospitality of her parents. In another early play, he depicted Thamyras, a great musician who challenged the nine Muses to a singing contest. If he won, he would be allowed to sleep with them all; if he lost, they could exact any penalty they chose. Unfortunately, he lost and was deprived of both his sight and his musical ability.

The Peloponnesian War and Sophocles' Later Career

Sophocles enjoyed a remarkably long and successful career as a dramatist. His ancient biography credits him with authorship of 113 plays. The implication is that he composed at least twenty-eight tetralogies, nearly one every other year from his *Triptolemus* debut until his death in 406. The same source credits him with twenty victories in the City Dionysia and adds that he often finished second, but never third. Among his also-ran tetralogies, however, was the one that included *Oedipus Rex*. It was beaten by the work of an obscure artist named Philocles, Aeschylus' nephew.

Of all his tragedies, only seven survive in their complete form: *Ajax, Antigone, Electra, Oedipus at Colonus, Oedipus Rex, Philoctetes*, and *Trachinian Women*. These are probably the ones that were selected for educational purposes by scholars of the Hellenistic Age, which followed the conquests of Alexander the Great.

Sophocles' early life had been spent in an Athens that was at the height of its power and prosperity. As time went by, however, the city's life grew more and more troubled. Athens had become an imperial power. With its seemingly invincible fleet, it secured the Aegean from the threat of a renewed Persian invasion. In return for this service, it exacted contributions in the form of money or men and ships (but mostly money) from the poleis of the Aegean and the Turkish coast. As time passed, the threat posed by Persia became remote and Athens' defense of Greek independence started to look like a protection racket. The Athenians spent the surpluses from its allies' tributes on the beautification of their city, including the construction of the beautiful marble Parthenon, the temple whose remains still grace the Acropolis today. When a polis attempted to secede from the empire, the Athenian fleet descended, besieged the city, and eliminated the dissidents. The statesman who directed the growth of the Athenian Empire was the Athenian aristocrat Pericles. Pericles was first elected to the annual office of *strategos*, or general, in 458 and was regularly re-elected for the next thirty years. His influence on Athenian politics, however, depended more on his ability to control the assembly through his oratory and his reputation for honesty and patriotism. According to the historian Thucydides, Pericles was virtually a one-man ruler.

Sophocles himself participated in the implementation of Pericles' imperialistic policies. In 440 he served with Pericles as one of the ten generals in charge of the war against Samos, an Aegean island that wanted to secede. According to his biography, Sophocles was elected to the office of general because of the popularity of his most recent play, *Antigone*. This was the first of three plays that he wrote about the family of Oedipus. It tells the story of how Oedipus' daughter, Antigone, martyred herself to obtain a decent burial for her brother (see Appendix 2). Though the earliest to be written, it dramatizes the final events in the Oedipus saga, ones that occurred after Oedipus' death.

Although he was a general, Sophocles' only involvement in the war seems to have been diplomatic, securing reinforcements from allies. Pericles himself handled the fighting with his usual efficiency.

The only independent polis that rivaled Athenian military might was the land power of Sparta in the south. Though the Spartans had enslaved their near neighbors, they were not otherwise an imperial power. They did, however, have mutual defense treaties with a number of poleis that had been discomforted by Athenian imperialism. In 431 BCE the Spartans and these allies declared war on Athens.

Led by Pericles, the Athenians welcomed the opportunity to demonstrate their strength. The Spartans and their allies needed to tend to their farms to survive and campaigned by choice only during the early summer. Pericles' strategy for dealing with the brief Spartan invasions was to bring all the Athenians inside the city walls, which extended to the harbor of Piraeus, and rely on the Athenian fleet to keep the city fed. He felt that Athens did not need its countryside. Meanwhile the fleet would also make amphibious raids on Sparta and her allies, who would soon find such a war unsustainable and sue for peace.

The strategy had a tragic flaw. Crowding the entire population of the Athenian countryside into the city created unhealthy conditions. During the second summer of the war (430 BCE), a plague broke out, arriving at about the same time as the invading Spartans. Thucydides' history of the war between Athens and Sparta contains a vivid description of the plague's horrific symptoms and devastating effect on Athenian life (Thucydides 2.47–54). The illness was prevalent for two years and then seemed to be dying out, only to return with a vengeance during the winter of 427/426 before disappearing once and for all (Thucydides 2.47.3 and 3.87.2–3). As thousands of citizens died, the Athenians continued to implement Pericles' strategy. In 429, however, Pericles himself sickened and died. It is natural to assume that he was a victim of the plague, but Plutarch's description of his serene death (*Pericles* 38) is inconsistent with Thucydides' description of the symptoms. In either case, according to Thucydides, the loss of Pericles' leadership led to Athens' eventual defeat in the war. It was the one contingency that he had not foreseen.

The Athenians may have seen a lot of themselves in Sophocles' depiction of Oedipus' Thebes. The play's action begins with a plague that forces Oedipus to search for a sinner whose presence is polluting the city and angering the gods. There is no evidence that any earlier versions of the story included a plague. It is a detail that Sophocles invented for his dramatization of the story. Moreover, the chorus attributes the plague to Ares, the god of war, who is attacking them, as they say, without his usual bronze weapons (lines 190–202). Plagues were normally associated with Apollo. The framing of the plague with the imagery of an invasion of bronze-clad warriors has no particular relevance to the situation in Oedipus' Thebes, but it fits Sophocles' Athens perfectly. The plague was doing the work of the Spartan invaders for them. In addition, Pericles was a descendant on his mother's side of the noble Alcmeonid clan. In the late seventh century BCE, an Alcmeonid magistrate executed the participants in a failed coup d'etat after luring them away from the safety of an altar at which they were suppliants. Because of that action, the entire Alcmeonid clan was found to be cursed and exiled from Athens, but they soon returned. In the run-up to the Peloponnesian War, the Spartans tried to embarrass Pericles by demanding that the Athenians cleanse the city by exiling the cursed Alcmeonids, including him. The demand was ignored (Thucydides 1.126–127). Still, no one in Athens could have missed the possible allusion to Pericles in Sophocles' version of Oedipus' story. Perhaps *Oedipus Rex* came in second because the judges felt that it struck too close to home.

Once the plague passed, the war unfolded as Pericles had foreseen. The Spartans and their allies were eventually willing to make a negotiated peace, but the leaders who replaced Pericles persuaded the Athenians to fight on in the hope of total victory. It was only after ten years of battle that the Spartans and Athenians agreed to a cessation of hostilities in 421. The uneasy peace came to an end in 415 when the Athenians, still seeking total dominance, launched an all-out attack on Sparta's ally in Sicily, the great city of Syracuse. The ill-advised and mismanaged invasion ended with the destruction of the Athenian fleet in 413. The loss of its fleet left Athens in a desperate situation, more vulnerable than ever before to attacks by Sparta and unable to control its subjects. Aristotle (*Rhetoric* 1419a6) mentions that a man named Sophocles was one of ten special advisors elected to recommend ways of coping with the emergency. It is possible but not certain that he is referring to the playwright, who was then eighty-three.

Sparta acquired its own fleet and renewed its attacks on a crippled Athens. The war dragged on at sea, with both sides, ironically, seeking help from the Persians. In the wake of a victory at the battle of Arginusae in 406, the Athenians once more had an opportunity for a negotiated peace and rejected it. The following year, their fleet was trapped and destroyed on the shore of the Hellespont by a capable Spartan general named Lysander. He then laid siege to Athens by land and sea, starving it into submission in 404. Sparta's allies wished to level the city and kill or enslave its inhabitants. The Spartans were more lenient. They required Athens only to give up its fleet, except for a dozen ships, dismantle the walls between city and harbor, and follow Sparta's orders in military matters.

Sophocles died in 406, without seeing the end of the war. For all of Athens' troubles, he seems to have flourished in old age. If *Oedipus Rex* was indeed written in the wake of the Athenian plague, Sophocles was seventy when he wrote it. Other later works include *Electra*, *Philoctetes*, and his last play, *Oedipus at Colonus*, which was produced posthumously. It is the story of the mysterious death of Oedipus. After long wandering with his daughter Antigone, he is directed by divine voices to a sacred grove in Colonus, Sophocles' birthplace. There he disappears in a thunderclap. He has become a heroic spirit protecting Colonus and Athens from its enemies, especially the Thebans.

We have a glimpse of the elderly Sophocles' wit and charm in a famous anecdote in Book 1 of Plato's *Republic* (329c). Getting on in age, he was supposedly asked whether he could still "be with a woman." "Shut up, man!" he replied, "Getting free of all that is the most pleasant thing in the world. I feel like I've escaped from a cruel, insane master."

Interpretive Issues

What's in a Name?

Our play's original Greek title was simply *Oedipus* (*Oidipous* for purists), which is what Aristotle called it in his *Poetics* (1452a25). Ancient scholars subsequently renamed it *Oedipus Tyrannus* (*Oidipous Tyrannos*), "Oedipus the Tyrant"—or simply "The Tyrant"—in order to distinguish it from Sophocles' other Oedipus play, *Oedipus at Colonus*. As we have seen, the Greeks did not necessarily think of a "tyrant" as an evil ruler; the term merely referred to a person who ruled a polis with absolute authority. Since hereditary monarchs with absolute power were rare in Archaic Greece, tyrants had typically gained power by means of a violent coup. Still, some of them were good rulers and champions of the lower classes. Yet the Athenians were proud of the fact that they had expelled a tyrant, the son of Pisistratus, in order to establish their democracy. Hence their view of tyranny resembled the early Romans' or the American founders' view of monarchy: okay elsewhere but not at home.

Since "tyrant" is unambiguously a term of abuse for us, it is usually avoided in naming the play. A case can be made for *Oedipus the King*, but "king" implies a degree of legitimacy that Greek tyrants usually lacked. *Oedipus Rex*, Latin for "Oedipus the King," is not a bad choice, since the image of kings in Roman literature and history is roughly the same as that of tyrants among the Greeks. I have used it because it is the title by which the play is most widely known.[1]

Hubris Breeds a Tyrant

Although "tyrant" was not part of our play's original title, the term is prominent in the text and thematically important. There is an interesting ambiguity in the way in which it is used. In at least two instances, it refers simply to hereditary monarchs: the stranger from Corinth tells Jocasta that the Corinthians want Oedipus to succeed Polybus as tyrant (949) and Oedipus refers to Laius as having been a tyrant (1043). In other passages, however, the term is used with the associations that it acquired in Archaic and Classical Greece: an ambitious individual who gained power through special effort. Hence Oedipus boasts of having acquired a tyranny (408) and taunts Creon by telling him that he lacks the resources to do the same (541). The instability in the term reflects the kind of dual reference that characterizes Greek tragedy in general. It is about both the mythical past and the author's own day.

The best known of the chorus's songs contains the famous line "Hubris breeds a tyrant" (872).[2] The song goes on to describe the inevitable downfall of the hubristic tyrant. Hubris in turn leads to an inevitable downfall. Here the later meaning of "tyranny" is in play. Hubris is an arrogant disregard for laws and other moral constraints. Since the typical tyrant of the Archaic Age gained power by means of a violent coup, which necessarily involved breaking laws, it was true as a general proposition that hubris bred a tyrant. On the other hand, power was freely given to Oedipus because he vanquished the Sphinx, and the chorus does not yet know, although they may suspect, that Oedipus killed Laius. The result is a long history of disagreement on the question of the relevance of this passage in the chorus's mind. Perhaps they intend their words as a warning to anyone who may be planning to overthrow Oedipus. On the other hand, what they say will turn out to be applicable to Oedipus himself—if one thinks that killing Laius was an act of hubris, which is a moot point.

As its imperial power grew, Athens' critics, and even some of its defenders, referred to it as tyrannical in its relations with its allies. The term was also used to tarnish the image of powerful statesmen, especially Pericles, and nothing stirred up the general population more than a rumor that someone was planning to overthrow the democracy and replace it with tyranny. Hence the possibility has been raised that the chorus's words about hubris and tyranny were not meant to be applied to Oedipus as much as to Athens or its ambitious politicians.

The Oedipus Complex

The long debate over the thought behind "Hubris breeds a tyrant" is typical. Sophocles' play is easily among the most discussed and debated dramas of all time. A recent work by a young scholar focusing on the question of whether Sophocles depicts Oedipus as morally flawed cites 1,125 different books, essays, and other documents relevant to the topic.[3] (The scholar's answer is no.) One reason for the interest generated by the case of Oedipus is that it looms large in at least two famous essays by great thinkers. One of them, of course, is Sigmund Freud. In his 1899 *Interpretation of Dreams*, Freud introduced what came to be known as the Oedipus complex. According to this theory, young children typically love and direct their first sexual impulses toward their mothers while hating and being jealous of their fathers. In normal individuals, these emotions are soon repressed and forgotten, but they still find expression in dreams and subconsciously motivated actions. Freud cites Sophocles' play as a literary work whose power is evidence of the Oedipus complex. He draws attention to Jocasta's comment (981–982) that many men have shared their mothers' beds in dreams.

Freud views *Oedipus Rex* as a drama depicting the irresistible power of fate. In it, he says, we watch spellbound as the hero's individual will is overridden by the supernatural forces of destiny. Oedipus would do anything not to kill his father and marry his mother, but he cannot escape his fate. More is needed, however, to account for the play's appeal, according to Freud. Dramatists of his own day wrote other tragedies in which heroes succumbed to fate despite their best efforts not to, and these did not have the same kind of power as Sophocles' play. The reason, Freud says, lies in the details of the story. In killing his father and marrying his mother, the protagonist is not succumbing to just any fate, but to one we all share: all of us are doomed on some level to love our mothers to excess and to hate our fathers.

Freud's comments do not amount to an interpretation of Sophocles' play. He does not suggest that the dramatist meant to depict Oedipus as the victim of an Oedipus complex. Freud merely cites the fascination accidentally aroused by the plot as evidence of the validity of his own theory of human development. That is an issue for psychologists to deal with in other contexts.

Fate versus Free Will and the Oracle of Apollo

Freud does say something about Sophocles' own understanding of his plot's inner workings, however. He assumes that the dramatist's overarching theme is that human beings cannot escape their divinely ordained fates. Indeed, the idea that you cannot escape your fate always comes up in discussions of *Oedipus Rex*. Is that what Sophocles means to imply? If so, what else is encompassed in such a belief?

Among the Greeks, belief in divinely ordained fates manifested itself in oracles and other forms of prophecy, which were ubiquitous and taken quite seriously. There were collections of ancient utterances by legendary prophets such as Musaeus and Bacis, roughly equivalent to Nostradamus. Through ritualistic consultations at temples, the devout also sought divinely inspired replies to their questions from priests or priestesses. The most prestigious of these sites was the temple of Apollo at Delphi on Mount Parnassus, where a priestess of Apollo, the Pythia, responded to questions posed by worshipers after prayers and sacrifice. Scholars disagree on the details of the procedure. It is possible that the Pythia went into a trance and that priests interpreted her incoherent babbling, distilling words of wisdom in the form of dactylic hexameters, the verse form used by Homer. Alternatively, the Pythia may have spoken normally and given straightforward answers that were later embellished and disseminated in the form of short poems. Oracles "edited" and distributed after their predictions had come to pass may have been the basis for Delphi's reputation for supernatural wisdom. In either case, the advice of Delphi was sought not only by individuals but also by delegates representing city-states facing weighty decisions.

Athens in Sophocles' day was a site of intellectual ferment, governed not by priests but by decisions made in the democratic assembly on the basis of public debate. The centrality of debate placed a great premium on the mastery of public speaking and gave rise to a class of professional teachers, the sophists, who taught their disciples how to argue effectively for or against any proposition. The first sophist to win fame was the brilliant Protagoras, who is still remembered for the opening sentence of his treatise "On Truth": "Man is the measure of all things." This motto admits of various interpretations, but in one way or another it tends to undermine the authority of supposedly divine inspiration. Another frequently quoted fragment of Protagoras' writing points in the same direction. "About the gods," he wrote, "I cannot know whether they exist or not, nor what they are like in form. Many things prevent such knowledge: the subject's obscurity, and the brevity of life."[4]

Protagoras and the other sophists were idolized in some quarters in Athens, commanding huge fees for lectures and private lessons. Others viewed their agnosticism with alarm. From the earliest times prophecy played an integral role in the Greeks' religious beliefs: unlike us, they could scarcely conceive of a religious person who did not believe in at least some prophecies. In this respect, Sophocles' own attitude was probably similar to that of his chorus: aware that faith in oracles is waning but hoping that the prophecies about Oedipus will be vindicated in some way (897–910). Otherwise, they will have to abandon holy places altogether. In terms of Sophocles' own times, the holy places whose prestige were at stake included the sites of the great religious festivals like the competitions at Olympia in honor of Zeus and magnificent temples like Athens' own Parthenon. In other words, much more was involved than the isolated question of belief in fortune-telling. As a result, some very thoughtful people, Sophocles among them, apparently clung to the belief that there was something to oracles.[5]

Belief in oracles implies that human actions are predetermined and can in principle be foretold by "seers." That in turn suggests an inhuman world view. Given the power of fate, what becomes of free will and responsibility? What's the point of praise or blame? The question was not foreign to Sophocles and his audience. In *Oedipus at Colonus* (968–973), Oedipus indignantly asks Creon how he could be held responsible for actions that were foretold before he was even conceived. Of course, a possible reply is that there is a difference between foretelling an event and making it happen. Yet it is impossible to understand how even the gods could foretell the outcome of choices that are truly free and undetermined before they are made. The priestess of Apollo at Delphi did not say that Oedipus was *likely* to kill his father and marry his mother, but that it was *necessary* that he do so.

A famous quotation by the Greek philosopher Heraclitus, who lived around the beginning of the fifth century BCE, seems to explain how the Greeks resolved the conflict between fate and responsibility. Heraclitus is quoted as saying (fragment 119) that a man's "character is his fate." The word translated as "fate" is *daimon*, which can denote any supernatural being but is especially used of a guardian deity that guides an individual along his or her fated path. Because of the frequency of that usage, it is sometimes interchangeable with the abstract term for fate or destiny, *moira*, and that is how Heraclitus uses it.[6] He is saying that our destinies are determined not by supernatural beings but by our own choices. Those in turn, however, inevitably reflect our inborn characters. No outside force made Oedipus do any of the things that he did. His actions were the products of his own will, and he is morally responsible for them. On the other hand, given his character, the sort of person he was, it was impossible for him to act in any other way. In that sense, we all have inescapable fates. We make the choices that we do and must endure their consequences because we are the way we are, and there is no escape from that.

Aristotle's Poetics and Oedipus' Tragic Flaw

To say that Oedipus is responsible for his actions raises a further question: were his actions blameworthy? This is the notorious question mentioned above as one to which an incredible amount of scholarly writing has been devoted—in part because the answer is critical to understanding the theory of tragedy that Aristotle outlines in his *Poetics*, the other famous essay in which this play plays a pivotal role. Writing nearly a century after the first production of the *Oedipus Rex*, Aristotle mentions Sophocles' play repeatedly as an exemplary tragedy (*Poetics* 1452a24, 1453a10, 1453b7, 1455a18). In the theory that he develops there, the ideal tragic hero, exemplified by Oedipus, is one who suffers misfortune because of a *hamartia*, an error or mistake (*Poetics* 1453a9–15). Scholars are divided on the precise meaning of *hamartia*. One school of thought holds that in the *Poetics hamartia* connotes an innocent mistake based on ignorance of a particular fact. In Oedipus' case, his innocent mistakes consisted of killing an apparent stranger who turned out to be his own father and marrying an unknown woman who was actually his mother. He cannot be blamed for the sins of patricide and incest because he did not know what he was doing.

The opposing point of view, less prevalent in recent years, is based on the assumption that *hamartia* can refer to a mistake arising from a flaw in character such as pride or anger, as well as a mistake stemming from unavoidable ignorance. On this view,

Oedipus' misfortunes were caused by defects in his character that are on display throughout the play, namely the tendency to lose his temper and jump to conclusions. His killing of Laius is just another example of his intemperate behavior. So it was really by his own fault that he killed his father.

Sophocles provides us with Oedipus' own description of his encounter with Laius (800–813). As detailed as it is, it is difficult to say whether Oedipus was acting in self-defense, the way any self-respecting hero would under the circumstances, or was indulging excessive anger. Oedipus says that members of Laius' party tried to remove him from the road by "using force." The crucial question, which the text does not answer, is "how much force?" Oedipus himself mentions that Laius' herald was present. Heralds were sacred personages deserving respect and specially educated to handle matters like questions about the right of way. It is possible to imagine that Laius' herald led a violent attack on Oedipus, so that he had to fight for his life, but a normal herald would surely have begun by asking him politely to step aside.

In the later *Oedipus at Colonus* (991–995), Oedipus defends his actions at the crossroads as a matter of self-defense, kill or be killed, but his perception could be faulty. During the course of *Oedipus Rex* (618–624), he becomes convinced that the innocent Creon is plotting against him and ought be killed. If he had acted on impulse and killed Creon, he would have called that self-defense too.

The trend in recent decades, however, has been to exonerate Oedipus. In a frequently quoted essay, the distinguished classicist E. R. Dodds pointed out that no one in the play criticizes Oedipus' behavior at the crossroads, suggesting that it was meant to be seen as normal under the circumstances. He also argued that Oedipus did not suffer because he killed his father and married his mother, but because he had uncovered his own past. Furthermore, Oedipus' investigation into his past was not foretold or predetermined. He undertook it freely and for the "highest of motives."[7] Hence his tragedy is not an example of a hero falling because of a tragic flaw in his character—on the contrary, he falls because of the excellence of his character.

I do not find such pro-Oedipus interpretations of the drama entirely convincing. To ask for Delphi's advice in dealing with the plague and then to follow its direction is depicted as a reasonable and decent course of action, but not a particularly heroic one. As for the elevation of his motives, Oedipus says at the outset that he wants to apprehend Laius' killer lest he himself become the next victim (139–141). In any event, he quickly forgets the plague and turns his search for the killer into an attack on Tiresias and Creon for their imagined treachery. When he returns to the matter of Laius' murderer, he does so in the hope of establishing his own innocence (834–837). It is understandable that some readers see Oedipus as a deeply sympathetic character, but he has some obvious warts. Sophocles seems to me to have deliberately designed his drama to provoke conflicting evaluations of Oedipus' character and actions. In fact, the differing judgments hinted at above are just a small sample. It has been argued by a reputable scholar that Oedipus knew that Laius and Jocasta were probably his parents all along and only staged his discovery of the truth.[8] An equally reputable scholar has argued to the contrary that Oedipus was not the son of Laius and Jocasta and did not murder the former; he was just tricked into thinking that he was and did.[9] It seems to me that everyone who reads the play or sees it performed encounters a slightly different Oedipus, and that is as it should be. Rather than creating an unambiguous depiction of a series of events implying one certain set of correct inferences, Sophocles has given us material for an open-ended conversation that may go on forever.

Notes

1. A Google search for the play's various titles produced the following results: *Oedipus Rex*, 395,000 hits; *Oedipus the King*, 185,000; *Oedipus Tyrannus*, 112,000; *Oidipous Tyrannos*, 16,000.

2. R. D. Dawe, ed., *Sophocles, Oedipus Rex*, rev. ed. (Cambridge University Press, 1982), 147–48, argues that Sophocles must have originally written "Tyranny breeds hubris" with reference to the fact that Oedipus, a thoroughly good tyrant in the past, has begun to act in a hubristic way.

3. Michael Lurje, *Die Suche nach der Schuld: Sophokles' "Oedipus Rex," Aristoteles' "Poetik" und das Tragödienverständnis der Neuzeit* (Munich: K. G. Sauer, 2004).

4. Fragment 80b4 in H. Diels and W. Kranz, eds., *Die Fragmente der Vorsocratiker* (Berlin: Weidmannsche Verlagsbuchhandlung, 1960), the standard text for the fragmentary works of early Greek philosophers. My translation.

5. The historian Herodotus, a contemporary and, probably, friend of Sophocles, says that he cannot reject oracles because some have proven so accurate and cites as an example a prophetic description of the Battle of Salamis by Bacis (8.77).

6. In *Oedipus Rex*, the chorus uses *daimon* to mean "fate" in line 1193. In lines 1300–1303, they ask what *daimon* oversees Oedipus' *moira*.

7. E. R. Dodds, "On Misunderstanding the *Oedipus Rex*," *Greece and Rome* 13 (1966): 43.

8. Philip Vellacott, "The Guilt of Oedipus," *Greece and Rome* 11 (1964): 137–48.

9. Frederick Ahl, *Sophocles' Oedipus: Evidence and Self-Conviction* (Ithaca, NY: Cornell University Press, 1991).

Introduction

Oedipus Rex

Characters

OEDIPUS, the ruler of Thebes. Oedipus grew up in Corinth thinking that he was the son of its king and queen, Polybus and Merope. He fled Corinth on account of an oracle that he would kill his father and marry his mother and was made ruler of Thebes when he slew the monstrous Sphinx by answering her riddle. He has reigned there for approximately twenty years.

A CROWD of Theban suppliants including young children and old men

A PRIEST OF ZEUS, king of the gods

A CHORUS of Theban elders, the town fathers

CREON, Oedipus' brother-in-law

TIRESIAS, a blind prophet serving Apollo, god of prophecy

JOCASTA, the widow of Oedipus' predecessor, King Laius, now married to Oedipus

A CITIZEN OF CORINTH, formerly a friend of Laius' man

LAIUS' MAN, a servant born in the household of Laius and Jocasta

A SERVANT who works inside Oedipus' royal residence

OEDIPUS' TWO DAUGHTERS, mute characters known from other sources as Antigone and Ismene

(The action occurs on the front steps of the palace of
Oedipus and Jocasta in Thebes. There is a grand doorway
in the middle through which the residents of the palace,
starting with Oedipus, enter the stage. Off to one side
there is an altar; a statue of Apollo, god of prophecy,
stands on a pedestal next to it. Of two side entrances,
one is for characters like the chorus who enter from
other parts of Thebes itself; the other is for those arriving
from the countryside or other towns, namely Delphi
and Corinth. A number of elderly men and young
children sit on the palace steps. An old priest stands in
their midst. Two youths who helped him mount the
stairs stand behind him. Oedipus enters.)[1]

OEDIPUS:
Children of Cadmus,[2] ancient king's new brood,
why have you taken seats before me here
as suppliants with olive boughs and wreaths?[3]
Meanwhile the city's full of fragrant smoke
and loud with sacred songs and cries of grief.[4]

1. I have provided parenthetical stage directions on the basis of hints
found in the play itself. There are no stage directions in ancient manuscripts.

2. Cadmus, a Phoenician, is the legendary founder and first king of
Thebes, Laius' great-grandfather. The kings of Thebes were Cadmus,
Polydorus, Labdacus, Laius, and Oedipus. During Laius' childhood, royal
power was exercised by a regent named Lycus, who was deposed and replaced
by Amphion and Zethus, sons of Zeus.

3. Suppliants are needy individuals who formally request protection or
some other kind of help from those in power. Suppliants in ancient Greece
carried olive boughs wreathed with bands of wool. Sophocles' words seem to
imply that these suppliants also wore woolen bands on their heads in addition
to carrying them on suppliant boughs.

4. Citizens were singing hymns, specifically those honoring Apollo as a
god of healing, and burning incense at altars as a way of soliciting divine help.

Not thinking it correct to hear about
such matters second-hand, I came myself,
the celebrated man called Oedipus.
But tell me, ancient sir—it's only right
for you to be their spokesman—what accounts   10
for this? Some fear or longing? I'll assist
in every way. He'd be a callous man,
who didn't pity suppliants like these.

PRIEST OF ZEUS:
My country's lord and master, Oedipus,
you see that we before your altars are
of different ages: some of us too young
to fly away, some weighted down by years.
I'm Zeus's priest and these selected youths
attend me. Others wreath their heads and sit
in agoras, Athena's double shrines,5   20
or where Isménus skirts prophetic ash,6
and you yourself can plainly see the cause.
The city's drowning now. She lacks the strength
to keep her head above the bloody surge.

---

5. The city of Thebes originally consisted of an area of high ground that
came to be called Cadmeia. In the sixth or early fifth century BCE, walls were
built encircling a larger area. It is likely that in Sophocles' day Thebes had
two agoras, or market places, and two temples of Athena, one on the Cadmeia
and one in the newer part of the city. It is, of course, anachronistic to import
this topography into the Thebes of Oedipus' day.

6. The Ismenus was a stream flowing through Thebes. According to
Pausanias (9.11.7–12.1), it passed near an altar to Apollo *Spodios*, "Apollo
of the Ashes," where divination was practiced. The ritual involved the
interpretation of chance remarks or noises. The reason for Apollo's cult title
was that this altar was made out of the ashes of burnt victims.

She's failing fast. The fruitful buds of earth
are failing, herds are failing, women bear
their labor pains in vain, and plague attacks,
the hateful fire-bringing god. He leaps
and leaves Cadmeia[7] empty. Tears and groans
have made dark Death the "wealthy one" indeed.[8]   30
These children here who sit before your hearth[9]
and I don't call you equal to the gods,
but think that you're the foremost man in life's
mishaps and reconciling those above.
On first arriving here, you rescued Thebes
from paying the cruel musician's deadly tax.[10]
You didn't get advice from us. Untaught,
but with a god's assistance, so it's said
and widely credited, you saved our lives.
We come in supplication, turn to you,   40

7. Thebes was originally called Cadmeia, after its founder, Cadmus, and later supposedly renamed in honor of Thebe, a minor goddess who married Zethus, King Laius' predecessor. See note 5.

8. Literally, "Black death is enriched (*ploutizetai*) by groans and sighs." This is a pun. *Pluto*, "Wealth Giver," was one of the titles of Hades, god of the dead, because of his association with the earth and agricultural abundance.

9. The hearth or central fireplace was symbolic of one's home. Suppliants sometimes sat in the ashes around a hearth, as Odysseus did when seeking help from the king and queen of Phaeacia in the *Odyssey* (7.153–154). Oedipus' suppliants, however, are speaking metaphorically.

10. A reference to the Sphinx. Sphinxes were monsters with a human head, an eagle's wings, and a lion's body. The one that visited Thebes was a female who asked passersby what creature had four legs in the morning, two in the afternoon, and three in the evening. When people could not answer, she killed them. Oedipus' claim to fame is that he answered the question correctly, whereupon the Sphinx killed herself. See Appendix 1.

the mightiest of mortals, Oedipus,
to find some means of safety, whether gods
inspire you or human counsel helps.
[We know most often men who've suffered trials
before provide the counsels that succeed.]11
Come, best of mortals, set the city right!
But carefully. We call you savior now,
remembering your former services.
We wouldn't want your reign recalled as one
in which we stood upright and later fell.   50
[Proceed with caution, set the city right!
Once omens smiled12 and you restored our luck.
Be just as equal to our present needs!
If you will govern here, the government
of men's a finer thing than ruling emptiness.
A vacant fort is worthless. So's a ship
without its crew, with no one living there.]13

OEDIPUS:
Poor children! I'm aware, not unaware,
of what you're longing for. I recognize

    11. Lines in brackets are ones that I believe are interpolations or later
additions to Sophocles' original text.

    12. More literally, "You restored our good fortune under a favorable
bird." At the beginning of an undertaking, Greeks often tried to learn
whether the gods favored their actions by examining various kinds of omens
or signs. Often that involved interpreting the appearance or behavior of birds
as expressions of divine dispositions. In fact, skillful prophets like Tiresias
could supposedly learn all kinds of things from the behavior of birds. Actions
that succeeded were said to have taken place under a favorable bird even if no
one had actually observed the birds at the time.

    13. See note 11.

that sickness touches all of you, but none   60
of you, however sick, is sick as me.
Your pain affects a single person, one.
You suffer selfishly, alone. I feel
the city's pain and yours and mine as well.
      You haven't wakened me from quiet sleep.
No, I've been weeping constantly for you,
exploring many winding roads of thought.
My search turned up a single remedy,
which I've pursued. Menoeceus's son,
my wife's own brother, Creon, went at my   70
command to Pytho, Phoebus's abode,[14]
to learn if something I can say or do
will save the state. I'm worried, measuring
the time. I wonder what he's doing there.

> (The priest's attendants have seen something of interest
> in the distance. As Oedipus speaks, they nudge the priest,
> who also looks with interest.)

His absence seems unduly long, but when
he finally comes then I'm no good at all
if I don't do whatever god commands.

PRIEST:
Your words are timely. These attendants just
alerted me that Creon's coming now.

---

14. *Phoebus*, the "Brilliant (or Shining) One," is a name for Apollo, god
of prophecy. His prophecies or oracles came through the voice of his priestess
in his temple at Delphi on Mount Parnassus. Delphi is also known as Pytho
and is "Phoebus' abode."

OEDIPUS:

O hear my prayer, Apollo, let him bring   80
salvation shining like his joyous face.

PRIEST:

It seems his news is welcome. Otherwise,
he'd not come crowned with berry-laden bay.[15]

OEDIPUS:

We'll be enlightened soon. He's close enough
to hear. Menoeceus's child, my kin,
what news do you come bearing from the god?

        (Enter actor 2 as Creon.)

CREON:

Good news, since troubles finally ending well,
in my opinion, count as fortunate.

OEDIPUS:

What were his words? I'm neither confident
nor frightened, hearing how your speech begins.   90

CREON:

If you would listen here amid this crowd,
I'll tell you now—or follow you within.

15. Bay trees, also known as bay laurels, have thick, glossy leaves. They were sacred to Apollo, and wreaths made of their leaves were worn by him in artistic representations and by people in various contexts as tokens of honor and celebration. Creon is happy that he has received a reply from the oracle that promises to end the plague.

OEDIPUS:
Speak out before us all. I worry more
for them than any personal concern.

CREON:
Then here is what I heard the godhead say.
Lord Phoebus orders us explicitly
to purge an evil growing up in Thebes,
not nourish it until it can't be cured.

OEDIPUS:
What sort of purging? How should we proceed?

CREON:
We have to drive a killer out or pay
for death with death. The city's drenched in blood.   100

OEDIPUS:
Did he reveal the murder victim's name?

CREON:
Before you set the city straight, my lord,
another leader, Laius, ruled the land.

OEDIPUS:
I know by hearsay. Never saw him, though.

CREON:
Our orders are in no uncertain terms
to punish his cold-blooded murderers.

OEDIPUS:
But where to look? How can the faded tracks
of ancient crime be rediscovered now?

CREON:
This land has answers, so he said. You catch   110
what's sought. The disregarded thing escapes.

OEDIPUS:
Did Laius meet his bloody end at home,
in open fields, or traveling abroad?

CREON:
He led a sacred embassy, they said,
departing Thebes and never coming back.

OEDIPUS:
No messenger or fellow traveler
returned, from whom some knowledge might be gained?

CREON:
A lone survivor fled in fear, but he
knew nothing, save one isolated fact.

OEDIPUS:
Which fact? A single fact can lead to rich   120
discoveries—to seize a slender hope.

CREON:
He said that robbers met by chance, not one,
a massive force, attacked and murdered him.

OEDIPUS:
How could a brigand be so bold unless
he made a deal involving silver here?[16]

16. As is pointed out in the scholia (anonymous footnotes on ancient

CREON:
That crossed our minds, but after Laius died,
we lacked a leader. Times were very hard.

OEDIPUS:
A tyranny[17] had fallen! What new ill
prevented you from finding out the truth?

CREON:
The Sphinx's singing[18] turned our minds to what   130
lay underfoot,[19] not solving mysteries.

OEDIPUS:
Then I'll uncover all of it again.
It's right of Phoebus, also right of you,
to show this dead man special courtesy.
Therefore you'll see me join the righteous fight
to help the country's cause and serve the god.
It's not a case of helping distant friends.
I'll purify the country for myself.
Whoever murdered Laius might decide

---

manuscripts), this remark seems aimed at Creon. Oedipus might suspect that
Creon hired an assassin so that he would inherit the throne.

17. It is important to remember throughout the play that "tyrant" and
"tyranny" were not pejorative terms. A tyrant was an absolute ruler. In Archaic
and Classical Greece, "tyrant" was applied mostly to those who gained control
of a polis by a violent coup. In *Oedipus Rex*, however, it is also applied to
Polybus and Laius, the legitimate hereditary kings of Corinth and Thebes,
respectively, and to Oedipus, whose situation is unique.

18. On the Sphinx, see note 10.

19. Throughout the play, Sophocles favors images involving feet. He is
playing on the name "Oedipus," which may be understood as containing the
words *oidein* ("to swell") or *oida* ("I have seen" or "I know") and *pous* ("foot").

to lay his violent hands on me as well.   140
I stand to benefit from doing this.
    You children, look alive, get up and leave
my steps, and take those olive twigs away.
Let someone bring the men of Cadmus here.
I'll handle everything, and with the god
we'll find our fortune fair—or slip and fall.

PRIEST:
Yes, rise, my children. His decree fulfills
the purposes for which we gathered here.
May Phoebus, having sent the oracle,
become our savior now and end the plague!   150

(The chorus of fifteen enters the dancing area at the
foot of the stage. They are young dancers impersonating
bearded men, the city's elders. They sing in unison,
dancing as they do.)

CHORUS: 151–215[20]
O dulcet voice of Zeus, with what design   Strophe A (151–158)
have you come down from Pytho's
        golden shrine[21]
to splendid Thebes? My mind is wracked
        with horror,

20. Line numbers for choral passages correspond to the Greek text
rather than the translation. See Preface, page xii.
21. Worshipers at Delphi dedicated gifts to Apollo, including gold and
silver artifacts. King Croesus of Lydia was especially generous, donating 117
bricks of gold as well as many other gifts (Herodotus 1.50.2).

my limbs are trembling. God that
*   Delos bore,*[22]
Ah-ahh! Paean![23] *I stand in awe of you.*
Will you accomplish something strange and new?
Or will the years as they unfold
reveal what they revealed of old?
Will I lament? Will I rejoice?
Tell me now, immortal voice,
O child of golden hope.

Great Zeus's daughter is the first I name,   Antistrophe A (159–166)
Athena;[24] *next her sister, fair of fame,*
Artemis[25] *— the marketplace her throne,*
she guards our native land as if her own —
and Phoebus striking from afar — you three,
allies in mortal danger, come to me.
If ever in some former year,
with deadly ruin drawing near,
the three of you did not refrain

22. Apollo was said to have been born on the tiny island of Delos.

23. In Homer, Paean was a minor healing god, Olympus' physician (cf. *Iliad* 5.401, 899–900), but the word was also used as a common noun to denote a joyous hymn of praise (cf. *Iliad* 1.473), the use that survives in English. In later authors, as here, Paean lost his status as a separate deity and became a name for Apollo when viewed in his role as a healing god.

24. Athena, Zeus' daughter by Metis (Wisdom), is a great goddess associated with skill in warfare, the domestic arts such as weaving, and practical intelligence generally.

25. Artemis, the daughter of Zeus and Apollo's full sister, is a goddess of wildlife and hunting. Pausanias (9.17.1) mentions a temple in Thebes dedicated to Artemis *Eukleia*, the "Fair-famed."

from banishing the burning pain,
then come again, I pray.[26]

Alas, my pains are infinite,   Strophe B (167–176)
all the host is ill.
And there's no weapon in my wit.
I've no defender's skill.

Our famous land is barren earth;
its ample harvests fail.
Women labor, giving birth,
but all to no avail.

One here, one there. It's all the same.
You see them rise and soar
like birds or some relentless flame
to reach the dark god's shore.[27]

Countlessly, the city dies.   Antistrophe B (177–186)
No compassion's found.
A deadly generation lies
unpitied on the ground.

Wives and mothers, young and old,
lament by altar's shore
pains and sufferings untold.
Their mournful voices soar.

26. This may be an allusion to two major outbreaks of plague in Athens at the time in which Sophocles wrote. See Introduction, pages xxv–xxvi.

27. The "dark god" is Hades, god of the dead. His kingdom is sometimes imagined to be in the far west, in a region of perpetual darkness beyond the sunset.

Their brilliant hymn and cries combine.
Zeus's daughter, please,
golden girl, O send benign
encouragement to these.

May Ares[28] *charging boisterously,*   Strophe C (187–202)
without a brazen shield in hand
but fierce with heat that scorches me,
reverse his steps and leave our land

for Amphitrite's spacious room,[29]
or harbor-hostile Thracian seas.
What nights release the days consume.[30]
O father Zeus, destroy him please,
hurl your fire-bearing rods.

Lycéan lord,[31] *I would exalt*   Antistrophe C (203–215)
your arrows shot from golden twine,

28. Ares is the son of Zeus and his wife, Hera. A god of war, he is depicted less sympathetically than the warrior goddess Athena. Whereas she is the patron and symbol of warriors who fight with intelligence and honor, Ares embodies pure rage and violence.

29. Amphitrite is the goddess of the sea, the wife of the sea-god Poseidon. Her "spacious room" would be the sea itself, i.e., the Mediterranean, whereas "Thracian seas" refers to northern waters: the northern Aegean, the Sea of Marmara, and the Black Sea. The chorus is just praying that Ares will go far away.

30. A mysterious line, literally: "For if night releases anything, it comes to completion by day." Perhaps the idea is that Ares presses his attack both day and night. If a person survives the night, he or she dies the next day.

31. Apollo is the Lycéan lord. The epithet indicates a connection with wolves (*lykoi*). In Sophocles' *Electra* (6), Apollo is called *lykoktonos*,

our best defense against assault,
and Artemis's blazing pine,[32]

with which she streaks the Lycian crest.[33]
O Maenads' mate,[34] *land's eponym,*[35]
Bacchus,[36] *golden-crowned, possessed,*
hurl your flaming torch at him,
the god despised by other gods.[37]

"wolf-slayer." The title may hark back to more primitive times when a major function of Apollo was to protect herds and herdsmen from predators. There is no etymological connection between the term Lycéan in this line and the reference to the region of Lycia below. There are many examples in the Greek of successive stanzas echoing each other's language.

32. Artemis' "blazing pine" is her torch. Pine trees and their pitch were and still are used to make torches.

33. Lycia was a region in southern Turkey where there was an important oracular temple of Apollo. Hence Apollo is sometimes called "Lycian" (e.g., Pindar *Pythian* 1.39). Here the chorus imagines the huntress Artemis, Apollo's sister, running around the hills in the vicinity of her brother's temple by night, carrying a torch. Sophocles probably chose the location just to echo "Lycéan" in the previous stanza.

34. The term "maenad" means a mad person. The Maenads were the ecstatic female followers of Bacchus, also known as Dionysus, god of wine and drunken revelry. He was the "Maenads' mate."

35. An eponym is a person whose name has become synonymous with a place or era; e.g., the "land of Lincoln," the "age of Augustus." Bacchus was the son of Zeus and the Theban princess Semele, Cadmus' daughter. Hence Thebes was sometimes referred to as the city of Bacchus.

36. See note 34.

37. This is true enough. In the *Iliad* (5.889–898), for example, Zeus berates Ares as a troublemaker, calling him the most hateful of all the gods. In the *Odyssey* (8.266–366), he is caught sleeping with another god's wife, Aphrodite, goddess of love, who was married to Hephaestus, the divine blacksmith.

(The chorus comes to rest, taking seats on the edge of
the dancing area. Their leader remains standing. Actor 1
as Oedipus has entered the stage from the palace during
the chorus.)

OEDIPUS:
You've said your prayers. Regarding them, accept
my orders, helping me confront the plague.
You'll scatter evils then and save your lives.
    To deal with this, I'll speak of something
        strange
to me, a tale and deed I've no connection to   220
and cannot find its trail without some clue.
For I'm a recent citizen of Thebes.
and so demand this help of native sons.
If anyone of you has knowledge of
the man by whom Labdacid[38] Laius died,
I order you to tell me who he is.
Don't even hesitate to bring the charge
against yourself. You'll suffer nothing more
unpleasant than a safe departure hence.
Or if you know about another man,   230
a killer from a foreign land, then speak!
You'll make a profit. I'll be grateful too.
But if you're silent, fearing that the truth
endangers you or damages a friend,
then hear the other words of my decree.
I now forbid that persons anywhere
that I am lord and master greet the man

---

38. "Labdacid" is a patronymic. It means "son or descendant of Labdacus,"
who was Laius' father.

whoever he may be, or speak to him
or let him offer prayers and sacrifice
or wash his hands in holy water. No!   240
He must be pushed away from every door.
That man is our pollution. That is what
the voice of Pytho's god[39] made clear to me,
and that being so, I join the battle as
the god's ally and murder victim's friend.
I curse the unknown man who did the deed
alone or helped by many. Let him spend
his evil life in squalid solitude.
And if my hearth is ever shared by him
and I have guilty knowledge that it is,   250
I call these curses down upon myself.
I order you to help fulfill these words,
for me, the god, and this our native land,
our dying, barren, godforsaken earth.

    Yet even if the gods were not involved,
neglecting such impurity was wrong.
When any noble man or king is killed,
the guilty party must be found. Besides,
it's I who gained the powers that were his
and share his marriage bed and fertile wife,   260
and if he hadn't come to grief, there would
have been the bond of common children too,
but fortune dealt his head a fatal blow.
For all these reasons I shall fight for him,
as though he were my father. Yes! I'll go
to any length to catch the murderer

39. Pytho is Delphi; Pytho's god is Apollo. See note 14.

of that Labdacid son, the heir of kings,
of Polydorus, Cadmus, Agenor.[40]

If any persons don't cooperate,
I ask the gods to give them barren fields,   270
and barren women too. Our present toil
or something even worse destroy them all!

You other sons of Cadmus who approve
these words of mine, may Justice join with all
the other gods to dwell in peace with you.

CHORAL LEADER:
Speaking as one to whom your dreadful curse
applies, my lord, I didn't murder him
nor know who did, but Phoebus having raised
the issue should reveal the killer's name.

OEDIPUS:
You argue justly, yet there's not a man   280
can force unwilling deities to act.

CHORAL LEADER:
Might I suggest a second-best approach?

OEDIPUS:
Don't even shrink from mentioning a third!

CHORAL LEADER:
I know most often lord Tiresias

---

40. Agenor, Cadmus' father, was the king of Phoenicia, which
corresponds geographically to modern Lebanon. On the other kings of
Thebes, see note 2.

sees eye-to-eye with lord Apollo. One
might learn a lot, interrogating him.

OEDIPUS:
Here too you'll find I haven't been remiss.
At Creon's urging I already sent
two escorts. I'm surprised he isn't here.

CHORAL LEADER:
We've also heard some murky old reports.   290

OEDIPUS:
Which ones? For I'll consider everything.

CHORAL LEADER:
That he was killed by certain travelers.

OEDIPUS:
I know, but no one saw the guilty man.[41]

CHORAL LEADER:
But if the killer has a speck of fear
and hears your curses, lord, he's sure to flee.

---

41. The Greek text as transmitted actually reads, "but nobody sees the
man having seen"; i.e., no one knows who the witness was. Since that
contradicts Creon's statement and does not sit well with the next exchanges,
which concern the murderer, i.e., the doer, and not the see-er, many editors
accept an anonymous conjecture appearing in an eighteenth-century edition:
"but nobody sees the doer." In Greek, this means changing *d' idonta* to *de
drônta*. My translation is based on that reading.

OEDIPUS:
Men bold in action aren't afraid of speech.

CHORAL LEADER:
There is, however, one he can't escape.
These servants bring the sacred seer now,
in him alone the truth has taken root.

(Actor 2 enters as Tiresias. Two youths attend him.)

OEDIPUS:
Tiresias, omniscient mastermind   300
of mystery and science, earth and sky,
although you cannot see, you're well aware
the city's visited by plague. In you
alone our only hope for safety lies.
In case you haven't heard the messengers—
when we consulted Phoebus, we were told
we must—to end the plague—discover who
Laius's killers were and either take
their lives or send them fleeing to other lands.
So don't begrudge the knowledge birds impart.[42]   310
Use every mantic[43] power you possess
and save the city! Save yourself and me!
Deliver us from murder's ugly stain.
We're in your hands. No work is fairer than
using your gifts to help your fellow man.

42. As a prophet, Tiresias was adept at interpreting omens, especially
the behavior of birds.

43. "Mantic" means prophetic. It is from the Greek word *mantis*,
"prophet, seer."

TIRESIAS (aside):
How dreadful wisdom is when wisdom brings
no gain! I knew these matters well but I
destroyed them.[44] Otherwise, I hadn't come.

OEDIPUS:
What ails you, man? You're looking out of sorts.

TIRESIAS:
Just send me home. You'll bear your burden best,   320
as I will mine, by heeding my request.

OEDIPUS:
You break the law withholding your advice!
That isn't what your city's friend would do!

TIRESIAS:
I've seen you hurling words that miss the mark.
I'd rather not commit the same mistake.

OEDIPUS:
You can't refuse to share your knowledge now!
Look here! We're all your humble suppliants!

TIRESIAS:
You're all shortsighted fools! I won't expose
my secret sorrows, not to mention yours.

---

44. An important line, rarely discussed. Tiresias says that he knew about Oedipus' crimes but that he destroyed that knowledge. In our terms, he repressed it. The passage introduces the notion of volitional ignorance, which could also apply to Oedipus.

OEDIPUS:
What's that? Are you concealing secrets? Why?   330
Will you abandon us? Destroy the state?

TIRESIAS:
I won't cause needless pain—to you or me.
Why question me? I've nothing more to say.

OEDIPUS:
You evilest of evil men! Do you
refuse to speak? You'd anger stone. How dare
you be so useless, so insensitive!

TIRESIAS:
While railing at my character, you miss
the one that dwells within to censure me.

OEDIPUS:
Who wouldn't lose his temper, hearing how
you show this city blatant disrespect?   340

TIRESIAS:
Although my silence covers things, they come.

OEDIPUS:
Your job is telling me of things to come!

TIRESIAS:
I'll say no more, so freely rant and rage
against my words. Let's see your finest wrath!

OEDIPUS:
My anger's such at least that I will not
refrain from stating what I think, which is:

you planned and all but did the fatal deed.
In fact, if you had any way to see,
I'd call the murder yours and yours alone!

TIRESIAS:
You'd do so truly? I suggest that you   350
obey your own decree and starting now
converse with neither these good men nor me,
since *you're* unholy. *You* pollute the land.

OEDIPUS:
And now it's brazen insults! Tell me why
you think you'll get away with saying that.

TIRESIAS:
I'm safe. I'm nurturing a mighty truth.

OEDIPUS:
And who's your teacher? Surely not your "art"!

TIRESIAS:
You—urging me to speak against my will.

OEDIPUS:
Saying what again? I need a better grasp.

TIRESIAS:
Are you obtuse or merely testing me?   360

OEDIPUS:
Your meaning wasn't clear. Please try again.

TIRESIAS:
The murderer you're looking for is you!

OEDIPUS:
You won't enjoy repeating lies for long!

TIRESIAS:
Should I say more to stir your anger up?

OEDIPUS:
Go right ahead. You're only wasting breath.

TIRESIAS:
Your closest ties bring infamous disgrace.
You dwell in evil you're too blind to see.

OEDIPUS:
You think you'll say such things in comfort long?

TIRESIAS:
If truth possesses any power, yes.

OEDIPUS:
It does—for any man but you, for you   370
are truly blind, in eyes and ears and mind.

TIRESIAS:
Poor fool, reproaching me with epithets
the world will quickly redirect at you!

OEDIPUS:
One nursed by endless night can do no harm
to me or any man who sees the light.

TIRESIAS:
Your fated fall is not through me. The end
is in Apollo's self-sufficient hands.

OEDIPUS:
Did Creon lay these plans? If not, then who?

TIRESIAS:
Your problem isn't Creon. It is you.

OEDIPUS:
O riches, tyranny, and art supreme,[45]   380
that ornaments the precious life I lead,
how great the envy is that we arouse
if loyal Creon, ancient friend, so longs
to gain the royal power that the state
conferred on me, a gift I didn't seek,
that he'd contrive a plot to banish me,
suborning this conniving sorcerer
this tricky mendicant, who has an eye
for profit, sure, but in his art is blind!
    Come now, if you're a prophet, where's the proof?   390
What happened when the rhapsode bitch[46] was here?
You should have spoken up and saved the town!
Her riddle wasn't meant for passersby
to solve. It needed your prophetic art.
And yet you didn't know the answer. Birds
could tell you nothing. Gods were silent too.

45. In Oedipus' view and that of Greeks generally, the supreme art, the master skill, is politics, which governs all others. The same view is expressed at the beginning of Aristotle's *Nicomachean Ethics*.

46. The "rhapsode bitch" is the Sphinx. A rhapsode was a performer who chanted ancient poems. The Sphinx is described as singing her riddle. In the Greek, she is referred to as a female dog, a term of abuse applicable—like "bitch" in English—to any disagreeable female.

but Oedipus, the ignoramus, came
and beat the beast with logic, not with birds—
the very man you're trying to banish now
in hopes of finding room by Creon's throne.   400
But you and he who plotted this will wage
a tearful purge, and if you weren't so old,
you'd learn your lesson now by suffering.

CHORAL LEADER:
In our opinion, both your words and his
were said in anger, Oedipus, for which
we haven't any need. We should discuss
how best to puzzle out the god's commands.

TIRESIAS:
Though you're the tyrant, I've an equal right
to answer you. At least that power's mine.
I'm not your slave, my master's Loxias,[47]
nor have I need of Creon's patronage.[48]   410
    You who belittled me for being blind
have eyes but do not see your evil state,
your dwelling place, or those you're living with,
nor even know from whom you came. You miss
the fact that you're your family's enemy

---

47. "Loxias" is another name for Apollo, like "Phoebus." It may be derived from the adjective *loxos*, "slanted, crooked," and refer to the fact that his oracles were never straightforward.

48. In Athens, foreign residents were represented in legal proceedings by patrons. Tiresias alludes to the fact that he is a native of Thebes, whereas Oedipus is (as far as he knows) just a foreign resident. Tiresias refers to Oedipus' apparent status again in line 452.

in life and death. Your parents' two-edged curse
is headed here on dreaded feet,[49] and you
will flee. Your perfect sight will darken then.
What harbor won't receive your frantic cry?   420
What Citheron[50] will not re-echo it?
Your balmy marriage will at once become
a hostile sea in which your household sinks.
A mass of other evils still unseen
makes you your father's equal, children's too.
So go ahead. Keep throwing mud at me
and Creon. Never shall a mortal man
be more completely crushed to bits than you.

OEDIPUS:
Am I supposed to listen to this rant?
To hell with you! Don't linger here. Just leave   430
the way you came. Vacate this household now.

TIRESIAS:
I'd not have come except you summoned me.

OEDIPUS:
I didn't know what foolishness you'd spout.
I hardly would have called on you for that.

TIRESIAS:
In your opinion, I'm a perfect fool,
but ask your parents. *They* would call me wise.

49. "On dreaded feet" translates the Greek adjective *deinopous*, which is
obviously a play on Oedipus' name, *Oidipous* in Greek. See note 19.

50. Mount Citheron is a limestone ridge between Thebes and Athens,
rising to 4,600 feet. It will be revealed that Oedipus' parents ordered that he
be left to die on Citheron as an infant.

OEDIPUS:
How's that? No, wait! Who *was* my father then?

TIRESIAS:
Today will be—and your destroyer too.

OEDIPUS:
You speak in riddles. Everything's obscure.

TIRESIAS:
I heard that you excel at solving them.   440

OEDIPUS:
Mock skill in which you'll find my greatness lies.

TIRESIAS:
That very skill, however, ruined you!

OEDIPUS:
It saved the city. That's enough for me.

TIRESIAS:
So then I'll leave. I need assistance, boy.

OEDIPUS:
Yes, let him help you leave. Your presence just
annoys me. Leave and spare me further pain!

TIRESIAS:
I'm leaving since I've said the things for which
I came. Your angry looks don't worry me.
They cannot kill. But ponder this: the man
you seek with proclamations far and wide   450
about the death of Laius stands right here.
Once called a "foreign resident," he'll be

revealed a native son of Thebes, but not
enjoy the moment. Blind, though born with sight,
a beggar, wealthy once, he'll use a staff
to steer his steps across a foreign land.
His children's father, children's brother too,
his mother's son and husband all in one,
he kindly helped his father sow his field
and killed him. Go inside, examine that   460
account and if it's wrong in any way,
then call my mantic inspiration false.

(Exeunt Oedipus and Tiresias.)

CHORUS: 463–512
Who is the man of whom we heard   Strophe A (463–472)
in rocky Delphi's mantic song,
whose bloody hands were not deterred
from crimes unutterably wrong?

It's time he use his foot for flight,
he must outrun a wind-swift horse.
Apollo's arms are hot and bright,
and he'll arrive in force.

Unerring Keres[51] *follow him,*
spirits that we dread.

---

51. Keres (pronounced like "carries") are winged goddesses of death, the
daughters of Night and sisters of the Fates. They carry away to Hades people
whose time has come, especially doomed warriors. They are "unerring" in the
sense that no one escapes them in the long run.

The snowy peak flashed its command!   Antistrophe A (473–482)
All must chase the hidden knave,
a bull traversing rocky land,
savage wood and sunless cave.

Wretched, sorrowful, and glum,
lame of foot and all alone,
he flees the prophecies that come
from Gaea's navel stone,[52]

but they're forevermore alive
and flutter overhead.

The wise bird-expert[53] *causes fear*   Strophe B (483–497)
and leaves my thought in disarray.
Agree? Deny? The truth's unclear.
I don't know what to say.

There's nothing settled in my mind,
for though I look I cannot see

---

52. Gaea (pronounced "guy-uh") is the great goddess Earth, the mother of the Titans, who ruled the heavens before Zeus and the Olympians. One of the sacred objects revered at Delphi was a boulder. According to Hesiod (*Theogony* 497–498), it was the very stone that Cronos, king of the Titans, attempting to thwart the fate of being overthrown by his own children, was tricked into swallowing instead of the infant Zeus. The stone was called the *omphalos* ("navel") and represented the center of the earth.

53. "Bird-expert" translates the unusual term *oiono-thetas* (*oiono-*, "bird"; *thetas*, "one who puts in place"; a *nomothetas* is a lawgiver). This is another reference to the study of birds as part of the practice of prophecy. Throughout the play, such references usually seem disparaging.

what's present now or lies behind.[54]
What is the enmity

between Labdacids and the son
of Polybus that proves the claim
the priest has made? I know of none,
and won't assail the name

of Oedipus to help avenge
some murders dim with time.

Though Zeus and Phoebus know and see   Antistrophe B (498–512)
everything that mortals do,
to say the priest knows more than me
is not entirely true.

One man's wisdom sometimes will
outstrip another's. That is all.
I won't believe the charge until
the truth stands straight and tall.

The winged maid[55] *attacked him then*
by day before our very eyes.
He proved a loyal citizen
and obviously wise.

I'd never want to think that he
committed such a crime.

54. For the Greeks, what "lies behind" is the future. They thought that the future was behind them because they could not see it, whereas the past lay, in effect, in front of their eyes.

55. The winged maid is the Sphinx, of course.

(Enter actor 2 as Creon.)

CREON:
Men! Citizens! I've heard alarming news.
Our ruler Oedipus denounces me.
I'm here in protest. These are troubled times.
If he believes I'd ever be a part
of plans to injure him in word or deed—
I wouldn't want to go on living with
a reputation such as that. It's not
a little slight, for nothing could be worse   520
than being adjudged the city's enemy,
an evil man, by you and all my friends.

CHORAL LEADER:
It's likely that his criticism came
from stress and anger, not his careful thought.

CREON:
Did he declare in public that the priest,
at my suggestion, manufactured lies?

CHORAL LEADER:
That's what he said. I couldn't tell you why.

CREON:
Well, did he have a steady gaze or seem
insane when charging me with that offense?

CHORAL LEADER:
I don't observe the way my masters act,   530
but he himself is coming through the door.

(Enter actor 1 as Oedipus.)

OEDIPUS:

It's you! You trespass here? Is your contempt
for decent feeling such that you intrude
on me at home though clearly having killed
that man and hoping now to steal my throne?
In plotting this you must have seen in me
some cowardice or folly. Tell me which!
Did you believe I wouldn't know that you
were creeping up on me, or not react?
But isn't it a foolish thing, to try   540
to gain a tyranny while lacking friends
and wealth? To capture one requires both.

CREON:

You ought to balance speech with listening,
then make a judgment based on what you learn.

OEDIPUS:

How fluent! Still it's hard for me to learn
from one like you, a grievous enemy.

CREON:

Just hear me out about that very thing.

OEDIPUS:

Just don't deny how evil you've become!

CREON:

If you consider stubbornness apart
from understanding valuable, you're wrong.   550

OEDIPUS:

Like you if thinking you can violate
familial bonds and never pay the price.

CREON:
I quite agree with you. That's justly said,
but tell me how you've suffered such abuse.

OEDIPUS:
You did persuade me, didn't you, that I
should interview a certain pompous priest?

CREON:
And even now I'd call it good advice.

OEDIPUS:
The Laius matter, when did that occur?

CREON:
What matter? I'm not following you now.

OEDIPUS:
When Laius disappeared. The homicide.   560

CREON:
The times involved are in the distant past.

OEDIPUS:
And was that prophet practicing his art?

CREON:
As wisely then and just as honored too.

OEDIPUS:
And did he ever mention me at all?

CREON:
He never did while I was there to hear.

OEDIPUS:
But didn't you investigate the death?

CREON:
Of course we did, but never learned a thing.

OEDIPUS:
Why was it, then, that wise man didn't speak?

CREON:
Where knowledge fails, I'm fond of reticence.

OEDIPUS:
You know and should at least acknowledge this.   570

CREON:
I'm always honest. Tell me what you mean.

OEDIPUS:
He never would have blamed Laius's death
on me if you had not persuaded him.

CREON:
You know the things the prophet said the best,
but now I claim the right to question you.

OEDIPUS:
You'll never prove that I'm a murderer!

CREON:
Your wedded wife's my sister, is she not?

OEDIPUS:
You've finally made a charge I can't deny!

CREON:
You share your powers equally with her?

OEDIPUS:
Her every wish is carried out by me.   580

CREON:
My rank is third--with equal power too?

OEDIPUS:
And that's what proves that you're an evil friend.

CREON:
Not if your point of view resembles mine.
Begin by asking whether anyone
would choose to govern, nagged by fear, instead
of sleeping well with equal privilege.
I've never wished to be a tyrant, just
to act as tyrants do. No one who knows
what moderation[56] means would disagree.
I'm not resented. All my needs are met   590
by you. I'd have distasteful duties if
I ruled. So how would that be sweeter than
this painless reign and dynasty of mine?
I'm not yet so deluded as to long
for something more than honorable wealth.
Now smiling faces greet me everywhere.

56. Moderation, *sophrosyne*, is a virtue of central importance in Greek
ethical thought. Its essence lies in striving to achieve the proper amount of
everything, neither too much nor too little. Creon's ostensible satisfaction
with being the third most powerful person in Thebes fits the formula well.

Those courting you request a private word,
and their success or failure rests with me.
Should I relinquish that for tyranny?
[Sound thoughts do not produce an evil mind.]⁵⁷   600
I've never cherished such a sentiment;
I wouldn't dare to help someone who did.
Now test my statements' truthfulness. Return
to Pytho, ask if what I said was true,
and if you prove I plotted anything
with that soothsayer priest, you'll have my vote
as well as yours to punish me with death.
But don't convict me absent solid proof.
[For carelessly mistaking evil men
for good or good for evil isn't right.]⁵⁸   610
To cast a noble friend aside is bad
as loss of life, one's dearest property.
In time, you'll second everything I say,
for time alone discovers who is just.
It's villainy that only takes a day.

CHORAL LEADER:
As one who's careful not to slip, I think
he's spoken well. There's risk in hasty thought.

OEDIPUS:
When foes are closing fast with secret plots
one's only choice is thinking quickly too.
If I should merely sit and wait, his plans   620
will be accomplished. Mine will go astray.

57. See note 11.
58. See note 11.

CREON:
What's your desire then—to banish me?

OEDIPUS:
Oh no! I'd have you die, not merely flee—
to demonstrate how evil envy is.[59]

CREON:[60]
You say you'll never be convinced or yield?
. . . .

OEDIPUS:
(I'll never yield to mortal enemies!)[61]

CREON:
You've clearly gone insane!

OEDIPUS:
                                    I guard myself.

CREON:
I'm equally involved!

59. Editors agree that one or more lines have been omitted in this area. The text as transmitted has Creon saying, "whenever you show what a thing envy is," which is difficult to fit into the context. My translation follows an emendation suggested by R. C. Jebb, reading the Greek for "in order that" (*hôs an*) for "whenever" (*hotan*). I assign the line to Oedipus, who is persuaded that Creon envies his position (cf. 381–386). He wants Creon to die to show to the world the ill effects of envy.

60. Some lines have dropped out. If 624 belonged to Oedipus, as I suppose, then Creon probably had a two-line reply.

61. My conjectural reconstruction of Oedipus' missing reply.

OEDIPUS:
                    An evil man?

CREON:
If you're mistaken?

OEDIPUS:
                    Still I have to rule.

CREON:
Not ruling badly.

OEDIPUS:
                    City, do you hear!

CREON:
I have some claim upon the city too!   630

CHORAL LEADER:
Please stop, my lords! Jocasta's coming through
the doors, a welcome sight, for she's the one
with whom you ought to settle this dispute.

(Enter actor 3 as Jocasta.)

JOCASTA:
What's all this senseless bickering about?
Aren't you ashamed, you wretched fools? While you
are arguing, the city's deathly ill.
Come in the palace, you and Creon too!
Stop magnifying your petty grievances!

CREON:
But, sister, Oedipus, your husband, means

to punish me with one of two decrees: 640
arrest and instant death or banishment.

OEDIPUS:
That's right. I caught him doing evil things
to injure me, suborning perjury!

CREON:
May I fare poorly, yes, and die accursed
if I have done a single thing you say.

JOCASTA:
By heaven, be persuaded, Oedipus!
Respect the sacred oath he just pronounced
for me and all the others standing here.

CHORUS (to Oedipus):   Lament (649–697)[62]
Be wise and change your mind, I pray.   Strophe (649–667)

OEDIPUS:
What's this concession you're asking me for?

CHORUS:
He wasn't foolish yesterday.
Honor the terrible oath that he swore.

---

62. Lines 649–697 constitute what Aristotle (*Poetics* 1452b24) calls a *kommos* ("lament"). It is a sorrowful passage in which the chorus and individual actors sing alternately. The actors also speak some lines, as indicated in the original by metrical changes and here by the alternation of italics and roman type. This *kommos* seems intended to show the chorus's distress at the quarrel between Oedipus and Creon. Their grief is what prevents Oedipus from taking action against Creon.

OEDIPUS:
You're sure of your desire?

CHORUS:
                              Yes.

OEDIPUS:
                                        Which is?

CHORUS:
Not to convict and cast out in disgrace,
on uncertain charges, a friend under oath.

OEDIPUS:
Just know that what you're asking for amounts
to seeking death or banishment for *me*.

CHORUS:
By the Sun, the most prominent god of all gods,[63]
may I perish completely, abandoned by gods
and mortals, if ever I thought such a thing!
And yet with the country so wasting away,
your quarreling on top of our previous ills
gnaws at the heart of this sorrowful man.

OEDIPUS:
Then even though it means that I must die
or be disgraced and exiled, let him leave.   670

63. It was appropriate to swear by the Sun, Helios, because he saw
all things and would therefore be aware of perjury. He was the "most
prominent" god only in the sense of being literally the most visible.

I'm moved by your unhappy face, not his.
He'll have my hatred anywhere he goes.

CREON:
You even yield with hate! Your anger's hard
to bear, but natures such as yours inflict
most pain upon themselves, and justly so.

OEDIPUS:
I thought you meant to leave.

CREON:
                              I'm leaving now,
unknown to you but fairly judged by them.

(Exit Creon.)

CHORUS (to Jocasta):   Antistrophe (678–696)
Aren't both of you departing too?

JOCASTA:
First tell me what was happening.

CHORUS:
Ignorant verbal charges flew.
Even unjust statements sting.[64]

---

64. These two lines are as strange in the original Greek as they sound in
this translation. Literally, they read: "An ignorant opinion of words came.
Even the unjust rends." The chorus seems to be saying that Oedipus
expressed his misguided opinions about Creon's treachery and that Creon felt
injured even though the charges were unjust. The obscurity of the language

JOCASTA:
And both were fighting?

CHORUS:
                              Yes.

JOCASTA:
                              The issue being?

CHORUS:
To someone concerned with his country it seems
sufficient to leave such a matter alone.

OEDIPUS:
It's come to this! For all your wisdom you'd
dismiss my case and blunt my anger's edge.

CHORUS:
Ah lord, and I've said this so often before,
I'd be manifestly insane and devoid of all sense
if I would abandon a leader like you.
Our country was lost, overwhelmed by its toils.
You steered us to port like a fortunate breeze.
We pray even now that you guide us again.

JOCASTA:
By gods! Enlighten *me*, my lord, and say
what action angered you to such a pitch!

---

may be attributed to the chorus's reluctance to disagree with Oedipus
too clearly—and to Sophocles' need to match the meter of the strophe
exactly.

OEDIPUS:
Since I have rather more respect for you,   700
I will: a plot by Creon, aimed at me.

JOCASTA:
Come tell me clearly what you charge him with.

OEDIPUS:
He says that I'm Laius's murderer.

JOCASTA:
He *knows* you are or merely heard it said?

OEDIPUS:
He had an evil seer spread the tale
to keep his own mouth wholly free of blame.

JOCASTA:
Then put your mind at ease regarding that.
Listen to me and learn a basic truth.
No human being possesses mantic skill.
I've brief but cogent evidence of that.   710
An oracle once came to Laius from
(let's say) Apollo's servants, not the god,
declaring that whatever child was born
to him and me would cause Laius's death;
but he was killed by strangers, so we're told,
some robbers, where a wagon trail divides.
The days my baby lived were scarcely three
when Laius yoked his feet and had a man
abandon him on pathless hills to die.
Apollo didn't make his words come true,   720
he didn't make my son a patricide,
and Laius didn't die the way he feared,

but that was what prophetic tongues foretold.
Don't let them bother you, for what a god
wants known, he'll simply bring to light himself.

OEDIPUS:
I suddenly felt dizzy, listening
just now. My thoughts are racing everywhere.

JOCASTA:
What's your concern? What startled you like that?

OEDIPUS:
I think I heard you mention Laius being
cut down by some divided wagon trail.   730

JOCASTA:
That's what was said. The story never changed.

OEDIPUS:
And where exactly did his death occur?

JOCASTA:
The land is Phocis.[65] Paths diverging lead
this way to Delphi, that to Daulia.[66]

OEDIPUS:
How many years have come and gone since then?

---

65. Phocis was the name of the region in which Delphi was located. It lay northwest of Boeotia, the region of Thebes.

66. Daulia is a small town about thirteen miles east of Delphi. The famous crossroads still exists. About twelve miles from Delphi, a traveler

JOCASTA:
The city heard the story just before
you came and made your powers evident.

OEDIPUS:
O Zeus! What's this? Have you been plotting too?

JOCASTA:
Please tell me what's the matter, Oedipus!

OEDIPUS:
Not now! I need to know how Laius looked.   740
Was he still young, enjoying his youthful prime?

JOCASTA:
His hair had only started turning gray.
A tall man, rather similar to you.

OEDIPUS:
Ah-ahh! I may have placed an awful curse
upon myself, not knowing what I did.

JOCASTA:
What do you mean? I shudder seeing your face!

OEDIPUS:
I fear the prophet isn't really blind,
but something else may cast some further light.

---

coming from Thebes can take a right turn and travel roughly the same
distance to Daulia.

JOCASTA:
I tremble, yet I'll tell you all I know.

OEDIPUS:
Did Laius travel light or, being a king,   750
command a company of armored guards?

JOCASTA:
He took a single carriage. Five in all,
counting the herald,[67] made up his entourage.

OEDIPUS:
The truth is now becoming obvious!
Who gave you all this information, wife?

JOCASTA:
A slave, the only witness left alive.

OEDIPUS:
Would he be here inside the palace now?

JOCASTA:
No longer. Coming back from there, he saw
that you had taken charge with Laius dead.
He took my hand and humbly begged that I   760

---

67. Besides being messengers, heralds were arbiters of ritual and etiquette,
charged with seeing that official business of whatever sort was conducted
correctly. The inclusion of a herald in Laius' party casts Oedipus' behavior in
a bad light. Presumably, the herald asked Oedipus to step aside in a manner
that was normal and appropriate under the circumstances. Heralds were
sacred personages; for that reason, the Spartans repented of having killed
Persian heralds on the eve of the Persian Wars. Cf. Herodotus 7.133–134.

would send him off to distant pasturelands,
as far from city walls as possible.
And so I did. As servants go, he well
deserved to have some even better gift.

OEDIPUS:
Is there some way to summon him at once?

JOCASTA:
There is, but why would you desire to?

OEDIPUS:
I fear that I've already said too much.
I think I'd better see him face-to-face.

JOCASTA:
He'll come at once, but surely I've the right
to know what weighs your spirit down, my lord.   770

OEDIPUS:
I've fallen prey to such foreboding that
I can't refuse. Besides, what better friend
to whom to speak at such a fateful time?
      My father ruled in Corinth, Polybus
by name; my mother, Doric[68] Merope;
and I was thought the leading citizen

68. The Dorians and the Ionians were the two great tribal divisions of
the ancient Greeks. The Corinthians were Dorians. Hence it seems superfluous
to identify Queen Merope as Dorian. Perhaps "Doric" should be interpreted
as a patronymic, implying that she was a descendant of Dorus, the legendary
founder of the Dorian tribe.

before an incident—surprising, yes,
but hardly worth the anger that it stirred.
We had a feast with flowing wine. A man,
a drunkard, called me illegitimate.   780
It bothered me all day. I barely kept
myself in check and sought my parents out
next day to question them. They angrily
denounced the man who let the story slip.
In that I took some pleasure. Still the thing
was irritating, always cropping up.
I made my way to Pytho secretly,
but Phoebus didn't dignify my plea.
He spoke instead of other dreadful things,
of horrors the future held in store for me.   790
He said that I would surely couple with
my mother, show to men a horrid brood,
and be my natural father's murderer.
At that I fled from Corinth's land, resolved
to use the stars to measure distances
and find some place where I would never see
the oracle's appalling words come true.
I came in time across the junction where,
by your account, that tyrant met his end.
With you, I'll be completely honest. I   800
had gotten near the triple path on foot.
A herald met me there together with
a man aboard a carriage drawn by colts,
like you describe. The leader tried to block
my progress using force. The older man
did too. I hit the driver angrily
for pushing me away. The older man
withdrew until I crowded past, then took
a double cattle prod and struck my head!
He didn't pay an equal price. In brief,   810

he felt the walking stick I had in hand,
fell backward off the cart and rolled away,
and then I slaughtered everyone. Now if
that foreigner and Laius were somehow
akin, is any man less fortunate,
more dogged by hostile deities, than me,
whom neither foreigners nor citizens
may greet or offer entertainment to
but have to shun? I placed those curses on
myself. Nobody else has any blame.   820
My guilty hands, which spilt Laius's blood,
have stained his bed. Am I an evil man
by birth? Is every part of me defiled,
compelled to flee this country, yet avoid
my native land and kin or else become
my mother's spouse and murder Polybus,
the man who gave me life and nurtured me?
I think it's only rational to see
in these events some savage god's design.
But sacred majesty of all the gods,   830
I swear I'll never look upon that day.
I'll vanish from the earth before I see
a stain of ruin such as that on me.

CHORAL LEADER:
There's cause for worry, lord, but cling to hope
until the witness comes and tells his tale.

OEDIPUS:
That is, indeed, my only hope. I must
await the shepherd. All depends on him.

JOCASTA:
What are you hoping for when he appears?

OEDIPUS:

Let me explain. My danger's passed if we   840
discover that his words agree with yours.

JOCASTA:

What did I say that carries so much weight?

OEDIPUS:

You said he spoke about some robbers, men
who slaughtered Laius. If he still refers
to *men*, I cannot be the murderer,
for one and many cannot be the same,
but if he mentions one unaided *man*,
the deed comes crashing down on me.

JOCASTA:

But rest assured that *was* his story then.
He can't unsay his testimony now.
I'm not alone. The city heard him too.   850
And even if he changes what he said,
he'll never vindicate the oracle
of Loxias, which stated that a child
of mine would be Laius's murderer,
and that poor infant never killed a man.
He surely perished long before he could.
That's why I haven't given any kind
of prophecy a moment's thought since then.

OEDIPUS:

And quite correctly. Still, dispatch a messenger
to bring the servant. Don't neglect the task.   860

JOCASTA:

I'll send him quickly. Now let's go inside.
You know I'll never act against your will.

(Exeunt Oedipus and Jocasta.)

CHORUS: 863–910
May fate find me accompanied   Strophe A (863–872)
by purity in word and deed,
revering laws that walk on high,
the children of the azure sky.

They were not born of flesh and bone
Olympus fathered them alone.[69]
They never nod with eyes grown dim,
or age, for god [70] *is great in them.*

Hubris[71] *breeds a tyrant. When*   Antistrophe A (873–882)
hubris satisfying its yen

69. The chorus is referring to seemingly timeless laws such as pro-
hibitions against patricide and incest. They propose a fanciful mythological
origin for such laws. They are the children of a father, Olympus (either the
mountain itself or a metaphor for Heaven, Ouranos), and a mother, the
bright upper air or heavenly ether, which I have translated as "the azure
sky."

70. As often happens, the chorus refers to "god" without an article,
which makes them sound like monotheists. In fact, the Greeks generally
believed in many gods but spoke of "god" (as we speak of "man") to denote
them collectively.

71. Hubris is the belief that one is above the law, an arrogant lack of
conscience. This is an important and controversial line, since it seems to
imply that Oedipus is guilty of hubris, an idea that many scholars reject. One
editor, R. D. Dawe, argues that Sophocles must have originally written,
"Tyranny breeds hubris." Given that reading, the chorus is saying that
Oedipus' position of power either has made him or will eventually make him
succumb to hubris. This is one of the many interpretive issues that each
reader must decide on his or her own.

for harmful substances ascends
the topmost beam to where it ends,

there must come next a sharp descent
that skillful feet cannot prevent.
God, keep the city in your grip.
I'll always trust your leadership.

May evil fate reduce to dust   Strophe B (883–896)
the man of haughty word and deed
who scoffs at gods and what is just
to satisfy his wretched greed.

How shall the man who profits much
but wanders from the holy path
and touches what he shouldn't touch
defend his soul from lightning's wrath?

If acts like those ennoble men,
why should I ever dance again?[72]

'Til these predictions prove their worth,   Antistrophe B (897–910)
I'll leave the holy shrines alone:

72. In addition to their value as entertainment, dances, such as those performed by tragic choruses, were viewed as a way of honoring the gods. The question is why the gods should be honored if their laws can be ignored with impunity. In these words, the chorus steps out of character as a group of elder citizens in Oedipus' Thebes and speaks as the tragic chorus that it really is.

Olympia,[73] *Abae,*[74] *and earth's*
untouchable omphalic stone.

Great Zeus, almighty in repute,
deathless sovereign, you should know,
men disregard the faded truth
revealed to Laius long ago.

Apollo 's everywhere denied
bright honors. Piety has died.

(Enter actor 3 as Jocasta.)

JOCASTA:
Lords of the land, the notion came to me
to visit temples where the gods reside
with holy wreaths and frankincense in hand.
For Oedipus is frantic, prey to pain
of every sort. It's quite irrational
the way he judges present things by past,
believing every frightful tale he hears.
My protestations fail, and so I turn
to you, Apollo, being the nearest god.
I bring these gifts and humbly beg your help.   920

73. Olympia in southwestern Greece was the site of the most famous
temple of Zeus—in addition to being the home of the original Olympic
games. The chorus seems to be saying that they will cease all religious worship
until Apollo's oracle linking the plague and the murderer of Laius is vindicated.

74. A town located, like Delphi, in the region called Phocis, Abae
(pronounced "uh-buy") was the site of another Oracle of Apollo.

Provide some pious way to end our grief.
We're at a loss completely, seeing the man
who steers our galley paralyzed by fear.

(Enter actor 2 as citizen of Corinth.)

CITIZEN OF CORINTH:
Could anyone, O strangers, tell me where
the house of Oedipus, the ruler, stands,
or better still, the man's own whereabouts?

CHORAL LEADER:
You see his palace, stranger. He's within
and she's his wife and mother of his sons.

CITIZEN OF CORINTH:
Then may she always prosper, she and all
her household, as befits his wedded wife.   930

JOCASTA:
The same to you. Your gracious words deserve
no less, but tell us why you journeyed here.
In need of something? Having news to share?

CITIZEN OF CORINTH:
Good tidings, lady, both for house and lord.

JOCASTA:
What tidings, man? Whose messenger are you?

CITIZEN OF CORINTH:
I come from Corinth. Things I have to say
will surely please, but also cause distress.

JOCASTA:
How so? Explain this twofold potency.

CITIZEN OF CORINTH:
The Isthmians[75] desire him to be
their ruler too. The word is spreading there.   940

JOCASTA:
Does ancient Polybus no longer rule?

CITIZEN OF CORINTH:
No longer. Death detains him down below.

JOCASTA:
What's that? Is Oedipus's father dead?

CITIZEN OF CORINTH:
Kill *me* if I'm not telling you the truth.

JOCASTA:
Attendant, run and tell our lord the news.
O sacred oracles, where are you now?
This is the very man that Oedipus
once fled in fear of killing. Now he's dead
by some misfortune, not by Oedipus.

(Enter actor 1 as Oedipus.)

75. The Isthmians are the Corinthians. The city of Corinth is located at
the southern end of the Isthmus of Corinth.

OEDIPUS:
Ah, there you are, Jocasta, dearest one!   950
Why have you summoned me outside the house?

JOCASTA:
Just hear this man and hearing give some thought
to where those holy oracles belong.

OEDIPUS:
Who is this person? What's he got to say?

JOCASTA:
He brings you news from Corinth. Polybus,
your father, isn't anymore. He's dead.

OEDIPUS:
Come stranger, be your own interpreter.

CITIZEN OF CORINTH:
If you require confirmation, sir,
I say the man is truly dead and gone.

OEDIPUS:
Did treachery or illness do him in?   960

CITIZEN OF CORINTH:
A little jolt puts ancient limbs to sleep.

OEDIPUS:
The poor old fellow died from sickness then.

CITIZEN OF CORINTH:
And simply having been alive so long.

OEDIPUS:
Amazing! Woman, why should anyone
respect the seat of Pytho's oracles
or heed the squawking birds above, when they
declared I'd kill my father, who is dead
and buried now, while I am here without
a weapon, innocent, unless he died
from missing me and thus I "murdered" him.[76]   970
No! Oracles are worthless. Polybus
has taken them to Hades, one and all.

JOCASTA:
And that's what I've predicted all along!

OEDIPUS:
It is, but I was driven mad by fear.

JOCASTA:
Now none of this should weigh your spirit down.

OEDIPUS:
Of course, I must beware my mother's bed!

76. In myth and legend, oracles were always fulfilled, but sometimes
metaphorically. Oedipus' remark raises the interesting possibility that he
might have avoided killing Laius literally if he had done so in some symbolic
way instead. Another famous story implies that he could even have slept with
his mother symbolically. Herodotus (6.107) tells us that before the battle of
Marathon, the exiled Athenian tyrant Hippias dreamt that he slept with his
mother and interpreted the dream as meaning that he would be restored to
Athens by the Persians and ultimately be laid to rest in native soil. Instead, he
lost a tooth in the sandy beach and fulfilled the omen that way.

JOCASTA:
What good can worry do a person? Chance
controls our fortunes. No one sees ahead.
What's best is just surviving day by day.
Forget about your mother's nuptials.   980
Many a man has shared his mother's bed
in dreams, and living life is easiest
for those who simply disregard the fact.

OEDIPUS:
All that you say would be convincing if
my mother weren't alive, but since she lives,
despite your words, there's every need to fear.

JOCASTA:
Your father's death is still a beam of light.

OEDIPUS:
Agreed. I dread the living woman though.

CITIZEN OF CORINTH:
What woman causes you to be afraid?

OEDIPUS:
The king's companion, sir, Queen Merope.   990

CITIZEN OF CORINTH:
And what's in Merope that causes fear?

OEDIPUS:
A dreadful, god-inspired oracle.

CITIZEN OF CORINTH:
One fit to tell or needing secrecy?

OEDIPUS:
It's not a secret. Loxias proclaimed
that I was doomed to share my mother's bed
and that paternal blood would stain my hands.
Therefore I've always treated Corinth as
a distant colony. I've prospered, true,
but seeing your parents face-to-face is sweet.

CITIZEN OF CORINTH:
And fearing that, you've always stayed away?   1000

OEDIPUS:
I didn't want to kill my father, sir!

CITIZEN OF CORINTH:
Suppose I end these worries, lord, what then?
I came to you in friendship, after all.

OEDIPUS:
You'll find me good at showing gratitude.

CITIZEN OF CORINTH:
And that's exactly why I journeyed here,
the hope of doing well when you returned.[77]

OEDIPUS:
I never will—while either parent lives!

---

77. A traveler who was first to arrive in a city with valuable information for its ruler expected to be rewarded. Such is the Corinthian citizen's ostensible motivation for bringing to Thebes the news of Polybus' death and Oedipus' election. By a wonderful coincidence, this same enterprising fellow played a critical role in Oedipus' earlier life, as is soon revealed.

CITIZEN OF CORINTH:
You clearly act in ignorance, my boy.

OEDIPUS:
How's that, old man? Become my teacher, please!

CITIZEN OF CORINTH:
You fled your family fearing what you said?   1010

OEDIPUS:
Afraid Apollo might fulfill his words.

CITIZEN OF CORINTH:
And sins against your parents stain your soul?

OEDIPUS:
Yes, that's the thing that always frightened me.

CITIZEN OF CORINTH:
Then nothing ever justified your fear.

OEDIPUS:
How could that be, if I'm my parents' son?

CITIZEN OF CORINTH:
You're not related, Polybus and you.

OEDIPUS:
He didn't sire me? Is that your drift?

CITIZEN OF CORINTH:
No more than I. Our credit's equal there.

OEDIPUS:
My father equaled some nonentity?

CITIZEN OF CORINTH:
I mean I'm not your father, nor was he.   1020

OEDIPUS:
Why is it then he always called me "son"?

CITIZEN OF CORINTH:
You were a gift these very hands conferred.

OEDIPUS:
And yet he loved me deeply even so?

CITIZEN OF CORINTH:
His prior childlessness had taught him how.

OEDIPUS:
Was I a gift you bought or something found?

CITIZEN OF CORINTH:
Found in the wooded glades of Citheron.

OEDIPUS:
What business brought you there, to that locale?

CITIZEN OF CORINTH:
My job was watching over flocks of sheep.

OEDIPUS:
A vagrant shepherd then, a hired hand?

CITIZEN OF CORINTH:
Your savior too on that occasion, son.   1030

OEDIPUS:
In what distress did you discover me?

CITIZEN OF CORINTH:
You ought to let your ankles testify.[78]

OEDIPUS:
Why talk about that ancient injury?

CITIZEN OF CORINTH:
You lay with ankles pierced. I set you free.

OEDIPUS:
I suffered infamy in swaddling clothes!

CITIZEN OF CORINTH:
Your very name recalls the circumstance.[79]

OEDIPUS:
O gods! My father's deed or mother's, which?

CITIZEN OF CORINTH:
The man who gave you up could answer that.

OEDIPUS:
I was a gift and *not* a foundling then?

CITIZEN OF CORINTH:
You were another shepherd's gift to me.   1040

---

78. Evidently, Oedipus' feet were still noticeably deformed from having been pinned together in infancy. That should have alerted Jocasta to the possibility that he was her long-lost son.

79. Oedipus' name can be interpreted as meaning "swollen-foot." See note 19.

OEDIPUS:
Which shepherd? Can't you make your meaning
        clear?

CITIZEN OF CORINTH:
He called himself "Laius's man," I think.

OEDIPUS:
He served this country's former tyrant then?

CITIZEN OF CORINTH:
That's right. That one was that man's shepherd,
        yes.

OEDIPUS:
And is that shepherd living? Could we meet?

CITIZEN OF CORINTH:
These local residents might tell us that.

OEDIPUS:
Is anybody here acquainted with
the shepherd being discussed? Has anyone
caught sight of him in countryside or town?
Speak up! The time for learning truth is now.   1050

CHORAL LEADER:
I know of only one, the man you sought
already, scouring the fields. But here
Jocasta's not without authority.

OEDIPUS:
My wife, the man we summoned recently—
is he the one this fellow talks about?

JOCASTA:
What difference could it make? Don't be concerned.
Don't give his statements any further thought!

OEDIPUS:
With clues like these there isn't any way
I won't discover who I am by birth.

JOCASTA:
I'm humbly begging you. Your life's at stake.
Give up! My sickness ought to be enough.   1060

OEDIPUS:
Calm down! Suppose I'm proved a triple slave,
my mother too. Your name's undamaged still.

JOCASTA:
I know, but listen, please, and don't go on.

OEDIPUS:
Not if it means I cannot learn the truth.

JOCASTA:
I only know and say what's best for you.

OEDIPUS:
If so, this "best" has tortured me for years.

JOCASTA:
I pray you don't discover who you are!

OEDIPUS:
Will someone bring that shepherd here to me?
Let her luxuriate in family wealth!

JOCASTA:
I weep for you, unlucky man. That's all   1070
I have to say. That's all I'll *ever* say.

(Exit Jocasta.)

CHORAL LEADER:
Why did the woman leave us, Oedipus?
She dashed away in bitter pain. I fear
that evils burst from silence such as that.

OEDIPUS:
Whatever needs to burst out will. I still
insist on seeing my seed, however small.
The woman has her feminine conceits.
She finds my lowly birth embarrassing.
But I am Fortune's child. When *she* is kind,
her gentle parenting brings no disgrace.   1080
If she's my mother, let my brothers be
the passing months. They made me small and great.
I'm me. I won't become another man
and falter at uncovering my birth.

CHORUS: 1086–1109[80]
If I'm a prophet, tried and true,   Strophe (1086–1097)
Citheron, the full moon's when
Oedipus will honor you
as mother, nurse, and countryman.

80. This short, happy song reflects Oedipus' strange optimism about learning the secret of his birth and provides the starkest possible contrast with the awful reversal that ensues.

We'll dedicate our roundelay
to you for all the courtesies
you've shown our rulers. Phoebus, may
nothing that we say displease!

Who was your mother, child, disclose.   Antistrophe (1098–1109)
A sprite hill-ranging Pan[81] *came near?*
A bedmate that Apollo chose,
to whom the tablelands are dear?

Was Cyllene's lord [82] *the one?*
Maybe Bacchus, holding sway
on mountain summits, found a son
among his bright-eyed nymphs at play.

(Enter actor 3 as Laius' man.)

OEDIPUS:
If one who never met the man can judge,   1110
the shepherd we've been looking for is here.
At least, this fellow's age would harmonize
with that conjecture. Add moreover that
the menials conducting him are mine.
But you're much better qualified to make
the judgment. You and he have met before.

81. Pan is the god of shepherds. He resembles a human being except for having a goat's horns, tail, and hooves.
82. Cyllene is a mountain in southern Greece. Cyllene's lord is Hermes, the gods' herald and the illegitimate son of Zeus. His mother, Maia, was a minor rustic goddess who lived in a cave in Mount Cyllene, where Zeus visited her.

CHORAL LEADER:
I know him very well: Laius's man.
No truer servant ever tended sheep.

OEDIPUS:
I'd better check with you, Corinthian.
Is this the man?

CITIZEN OF CORINTH:
                    The very one you see.   1120

OEDIPUS (to Laius' man):
Then pay attention, ancient sir, to what
I ask. Did you belong to Laius once?

LAIUS' MAN:
I did, a servant born and bred at home.

OEDIPUS:
What duties did you have? What livelihood?

LAIUS' MAN:
Most of my life I tended flocks of sheep.

OEDIPUS:
And passed your days in certain areas?

LAIUS' MAN:
Mount Citheron and nearby pasturelands.

OEDIPUS:
And did you get to know this fellow here?

LAIUS' MAN:
What did he do? Who's that you're speaking of?

OEDIPUS:
This fellow. Did you ever meet before?   1130

LAIUS' MAN:
I couldn't say right now from memory.

CITIZEN OF CORINTH:
That's not at all surprising, lord, but I
can help him recollect. He surely does
recall the times he grazed his double flock,
and I my single one, on Citheron.
From spring until Arcturus rose,[83] for six
entire months, we labored side by side,
three times. When winter finally came, he drove
his flocks to Theban stables, I to mine.
Did all this happen as I say or not?   1140

LAIUS' MAN:
It happened, yes, but rather long ago.

CITIZEN OF CORINTH:
Do you remember giving me a child,
an infant I could raise and call my own?

LAIUS' MAN:
What's going on? Why question me like this?

83. Arcturus, the "Bear's Guardian," is one of the brightest stars. It is
named from its location near the constellation Ursa Major, the "Greater
Bear." In the northern hemisphere it first appears above the eastern horizon
at dawn in mid-September. For the Greeks, its appearance marked the
beginning of stormy, winter weather. The Corinthian says, in effect, that he

CITIZEN OF CORINTH:
Good friend, that little child is now this man.

LAIUS' MAN:
Damnation! Can't you learn to hold your tongue?

OEDIPUS:
Old man, you'd better stop rebuking him.
Your words, not his, require discipline.

LAIUS' MAN:
Most noble master! Where do I go wrong?

OEDIPUS:
Not telling him about the little child.   1150

LAIUS' MAN:
He's ignorant! He's only wasting time.

OEDIPUS:
If kindness doesn't make you speak, there's pain.

LAIUS' MAN:
O gods! I'm elderly! Don't torture me!

OEDIPUS:
Enough delay! Will someone hold his arms?[84]

------

and Laius' man grazed their sheep on Citheron from March to September,
from the vernal to the autumnal equinox.

84. Oedipus' intention at this point is apparently to have Laius' man
flogged.

LAIUS' MAN:
Unhappy man! What *is* it you must know?

OEDIPUS:
You gave this man the child he's speaking of?

LAIUS' MAN:
I did and only wish I died that day!

OEDIPUS:
If you don't talk, you'll finally get your wish.

LAIUS' MAN:
I fear I'll get it sooner if I do.

OEDIPUS:
I think this man is bent on wasting time!   1160

LAIUS' MAN:
But I already said I gave the child!

OEDIPUS:
But gotten where? Your own? Some other
        man's?

LAIUS' MAN:
He wasn't mine. He came from someone else.

OEDIPUS:
Which house? A citizen's? One standing here?

LAIUS' MAN:
O master, please don't ask me any more!

OEDIPUS:
If I must ask you any more, you'll die.

LAIUS' MAN:
All right! The child was one that Laius . . . had.

OEDIPUS:
You mean a servant's child or one of his?

LAIUS' MAN:
Ah-ahh! I'm close to saying the awful thing.

OEDIPUS:
And I to hearing. Yet it must be heard.   1170

LAIUS' MAN:
They said that Laius fathered him, but one
within would tell the story best—your wife.

OEDIPUS:
She gave the little child to you?

LAIUS' MAN:
                                        She did.

OEDIPUS:
With what instructions?

LAIUS' MAN:
                                "Do away with him."

OEDIPUS:
His mother! Why?

LAIUS' MAN:
Her fear of prophecies.

OEDIPUS:
Of what?

LAIUS' MAN:
He'd be his father's murderer.

OEDIPUS:
What prompted you to give the child to *him*?

LAIUS' MAN:
Just pity. I assumed he'd carry him
away to foreign parts, to where he lived.
He saved the child—for greatest misery.   1180
If you are he, you're surely cursed by fate.

OEDIPUS:
Aa-ahh! Now everything's becoming clear!
O light—the last I'll ever see, I stand
exposed, all wrong in parents, those with whom
I lived and him I murdered, wrong, all wrong!

(Exeunt Oedipus and Laius' Man.)

CHORUS: 1186–1222
Spawn of mortal generations, hear!   Strophe A (1186–1196)
Your lives are nothing. Who of you can
        say
his happiness did more than just appear
and having done so turned and
        walked away?

If Oedipus's fate's [85] *the test,*
no human state is truly blest.

You shot a lofty arrow, unafraid   Antistrophe A (1197–1204)
to gain all that for which a mortal
      strives.
You slew the mantic, predatory maid,
became our fortress, saved our very lives.

Our highest honors as the lord
and king of Thebes were your reward.

But now who has a sadder tale to tell   Strophe B (1205–1212)
of cruel destruction, toil, reverse of lot?
Poor Oedipus, one harbor served you well
as child and husband, getting and begot.

How could the field your father plowed,
when plowed by you, not cry aloud?

Time seeing all things, exposing you   Antistrophe B (1213–1222)
      at last,
condemns the monstrous troth of
      sire-son.
I wish I'd never seen you. I'm aghast.
I weep and wail, and yet you are the one

---

85. The Greek word translated as "fate" is *daimon*. Its primary meaning is "supernatural being," i.e., anything from a major god to an anonymous spirit. It is especially used, however, of a lesser deity that supervises an individual's fate. Because of that association, it sometimes is used as nothing more than a colorful synonym for *moira*, the proper term for fate, as is the case here.

who once enabled me to rise
and drifted sleep across my eyes.

(Enter actor 3 as servant.)

SERVANT:
This land's most highly honored gentlemen,
if you still hold the house Labdacids built
in high regard, what dreadful deeds you have
to hear about and witness! What dismay!
The Danube merged with Phasis[86] couldn't
    clean
the building, such atrocities it hides
and will too quickly bring to light. These ills
were voluntary, not the opposite.   1230
What hurt the most are pains we freely choose.

CHORAL LEADER:
The facts that we've already learned are grief
enough. Do you have something more to add?

SERVANT:
The news most quickly said and understood
is this: the godlike Queen Jocasta's dead.

CHORAL LEADER:
Unhappy woman! How? What caused her death?

---

86. A river that flows into the eastern extremity of the Black Sea,
the counterpart of the Danube on the west. The city of Colchis, where
Jason sailed to obtain the Golden Fleece, was located at the mouth of
the Phasis.

SERVANT:

She killed herself. The most distressing part
of what occurred is absent now: the sight,
but you shall hear the woman's sufferings
as fully as my memory allows.   1240
She passed inside the hall in passion's grip,
tearing her hair with all her fingers' might,
and went directly toward her marriage bed.
Arriving there, she slammed the bedroom doors
and called on Laius, dead for years, a corpse.
She recollected times he "planted seeds
by which he perished," leaving her "to bear
his offspring misbegotten progeny."
She cursed her bed: she bore "a husband by
her husband there and children by her child."   1250
I can't describe what happened next, her death,
for Oedipus came bursting in with shouts,
preventing us from seeing her suffering.
Instead we watched him lurching round the hall.
He ordered us to fetch his sword and find
his wife, "though less a wife than double field,
maternal soil, his own, and children's too."
Mad as he was, some spirit showed the way,
for no one standing close at hand had dared.
As if some force directed him, he yelled   1260
and crashed against the double doors until
he bent the bars and tumbled in the room.
That's when we saw Jocasta hanging there,
ensnared in woven ropes. He saw her too.
His groan was like a wounded animal's.
Untying the noose, he laid his woman down.
What happened next was horrible to see.
She wore a gown with brooches made of gold.
He took them off her shoulders, raised them high

and struck the rounded sockets of his eyes.   1270
He cried that they would never look upon
the evils he'd experienced or done.
He'd see forbidden faces darkly now
and those he should have known would
           vanish too.
Meanwhile the brooches never ceased to rise
and fall. He struck his eyes so many times
his face was soaking wet with blood that poured
from them, and not a sprinkling here and there,
a blinding storm, a hurricane of gore.
These evils didn't break from him alone.   1280
A man and woman's partnership was cause.
The happiness they had in former years
was truly happiness, but now, today,
disgrace and ruin, lamentation, death
—no evil you can name has stayed away.

CHORAL LEADER:
Has that poor man found any peace of mind?

SERVANT:
He's shouting now to part the doors and show
to Thebes a father-killer who . . . but no,
I can't repeat his sacrilegious words.
He'll make himself an outcast, not remain
at home accursed by curses he proclaimed.   1290
But even so he needs a steady guide.
So great a sickness can't be borne alone.
He'll show you soon enough. The palace doors
are parting. Presently, you'll see a sight
to move a bitter enemy to tears.

           (Enter actor 1 as Oedipus blind.)

CHORUS: Lament (1297–1366)[87]

O dreadful suffering to see,
most dreadful sight beneath the sun,
what is this wild insanity 1300
assaulting you, unhappy one?
What power leaping from the skies
oversees your wretched fate?
Pheu! Pheu![88] I turn my eyes,
although there's much to contemplate.
and many questions do arise.
The horror you cause is much too great.

OEDIPUS:

Ah-ahh! Ah-ahh! How wretched am I!
Where in the world are you carrying me?
Where does my utterance, borne about, fly? 1310
Where have you vaulted—eeoh!—Destiny?[89]

CHORUS:
Some dreadful place, unfit to hear or see.

OEDIPUS:

O loathsome dark that won't recede,
O foul fair wind against my back,
the sharp pangs of my recent deed
and evil memories attack!

87. Another *kommos*. See note 62.

88. *Pheu!* is a Greek interjection expressing grief and anger. In my translation, I treat it as a disyllable, "Phay-oo, phay-oo!"

89. Oedipus uses the word *daimon* for destiny (or fate). See note 85. "*Eeoh*" transliterates the interjection that precedes *daimon* in Greek. It is a cry of distress used when invoking gods.

CHORUS:
Amid such sorrow, it's no wonder that
you doubly grieve and feel a double pain.   1320

OEDIPUS:
My friend! Now only you are here
To care for one who's lost his sight.
You don't escape. Your voice is clear,
I know it through the darkest night.

CHORUS:
Of dreadful deeds you've done, how could
         you quench
your sight? What power put you up to that?

OEDIPUS:
Apollo caused all this dismay,   1330
but it was I alone, not he,
who struck my eyes. What good are they
when there is nothing sweet to see?

CHORUS:
I could not disagree.

OEDIPUS:
What sight is there that I hold dear,
what greeting I'd be pleased to hear?

Friends, drive me out and far away,   1340
eliminate the awful pest,
the man accursed, without delay,
the human being the gods detest.

CHORUS:
Your thoughts are sad as your misfortunes
        are.
I'd rather not have known of you at all.

OEDIPUS:
I curse the herdsman who untied
cruel bonds and saved my life. No gain.   1350
For otherwise I would have died
and spared myself and you such pain.

CHORUS:
I too would not complain.

OEDIPUS:
I'd not have killed my father then,
been called my mother's groom by men.

Now I'm the godless child who's been
in his unholy parents' bed.   1360
Whatever evil precedes sin [90]
Oedipus inherited.

CHORAL LEADER:
I wouldn't say that what you did is wise.
Prefer no longer being to living blind!

90. Literally, "if any evil is older than evil." Here Oedipus seems to
allude to the paradox that his acts were determined before he was born, and
yet he is conscious of guilt.

OEDIPUS:

Don't lecture me, insinuating that
my recent action wasn't for the best.   1370
I can't conceive what brazen eyes I'd need
to greet my father there in Hades' realm
or view my mother's grief. The things I did
to them make hanging seem too lenient.
Would I enjoy my children's faces then
and yearn to watch such blossoms blossoming?
That's not a sight my eyes would ever seek,
nor are the city walls and battlements
or sacred statues, all of which I'm banned
from seeing by curses I pronounced myself,   1380
once Thebes' most pampered citizen, when I
bid all to shun the sinner, whom the gods
have shown to be Laius's cursèd son.
While sporting such a filthy stain, how could
I meet another's eyes with steady looks?
If there were any way to block the stream
of sound that courses through my ears, I'd not
refrain from sealing all my sorry self,
being deaf and sightless too. How sweet to have
a mind that dwells where evil cannot reach!   1390
    Why *did* you shelter me, O Citheron?
You should have killed me quickly, then and
            there,
that I might never show my source to men.
    O Polybus and Corinth, native land,
as once supposed, you raised a lovely thing
in me, but evil festered underneath.
Behold an evil man with evil roots!
    O valley hidden where a trail divides,
three narrow paths amid the crowding oaks,

crossroads that drank my father's blood, my own   1400
and spilt by me, do you remember still
the things I did by you? My later deeds
upon arriving here?

                    O wedding days!
my wedding days! you gave me birth and then
reused my seed, and so the harvest grew:
fraternal fathers, single-blooded sons,
mothers in bridal gowns, and every sin
the human race has called most foul, and yet—
one shouldn't name unlovely deeds aloud.

    Act quickly now and drive me far away,   1410
or murder me or bury me beneath
the sea and never see me anymore.

    Step forward. Deign to touch my suffering.
Don't be afraid. No other human being
could bear my evils, only Oedipus!

    (Enter actor 2 as Creon.)

CHORAL LEADER:
Look! Here is Creon, just in time to act
or counsel us on your demands, since he
replaces you as Thebes' sole guardian.

OEDIPUS:
No! No! What words have I for Creon now?
Do I have any way to win his trust?   1420
I did him every kind of wrong before.

CREON:
I haven't come for gloating, Oedipus,
or criticizing you for past mistakes,

but if you haven't any shame before[91]
the sons of men, respect the fire that
sustains all living things, lord Helios.
Do not expose your foul pollution. Earth,
the pouring rain, and light of day recoil.
Attendants, quickly help him go inside.
It's simple decency that kindred folk,   1430
and they alone, should witness family grief.

OEDIPUS:
Your coming here, a man so good to one
this vile, has changed my expectation so
I'd ask a favor, more for you than me.

CREON:
What is this service you're so eager for?

OEDIPUS:
Make me an outcast now, exiled to where
I'll never meet another human being.

CREON:
I would have done so gladly. First I wished
to ask the god what action *he* prescribes.

OEDIPUS:
But his command was very clear. You must   1440
destroy the godless father-killer, me.

91. Dawe argues that the original end of the play is lost and that what we
have (i.e., lines 1424–1530) was written by a different, later author in order to
bring the story into line with Sophocles' later sequel, *Oedipus at Colonus*. The

CREON:
That's what was said, but given where we stand,
we'd better learn for certain what to do.

OEDIPUS:
Do that for such a wretched man as me?

CREON:
Indeed, and you must finally trust the god.

OEDIPUS:
I do demand and humbly pray that you
do something else. Provide the final rites
you choose for her within, as kinsmen should,
but never ask my father's city here
to welcome me alive within its walls.   1450
No, let me wander hills where I belong,
the heights that people call Mount Citheron,
the place my parents made my living grave.
I'll die the way that pair of killers wished.
      Of this, I'm very sure. No accident
or illness ever could have caused my death.
I was preserved for something horrible.
Let fate continue down its chosen path.
      About my sons,[92] you need not, Creon, give
them any thought. They're men and can secure   1460
their livelihoods wherever they may be.

―――――

quality of the thought and language of the text does seem to decline from this
point forward, but it is the only ending we have.
      92. Oedipus' sons are known from other sources as Polynices and Eteocles.
When Oedipus goes into exile, they fight over control of Thebes and end up
killing each other.

(Oedipus' two daughters emerge from the palace and slowly approach Oedipus.)

My poor, defenseless, maiden daughters[93] though —
my dining table never stood apart
from them. They never ate without me. All
the food I ever touched I shared with them.
Take care of them and grant my fondest wish,
to feel their touch while weeping grief away.
Oh please, my lord!
Oh please! You're nobly born. A touch would make
their presence real, as when I had my sight.   1470
What am I saying?
Do I not hear my two belovèd girls?
I hear them weep! Did Creon sympathize
and bring my darling daughters here to me?
Could I be right?

CREON:
Yes, I arranged their presence here myself.
I knew the joy they've always brought to you.

OEDIPUS:
Then fare you well, and for this favor may
a kinder fate attend your life than mine.
Where are you, children? Where? Come here to me!   1480
Come here to these fraternal hands, by whose
kind service your prolific father's eyes,
which used to glisten, see the way they do.

---

93. Oedipus' daughters are Antigone and Ismene. In *Oedipus at Colonus*, Antigone attends her father in exile and then, in *Antigone*, martyrs herself in the cause of securing a proper burial for her brother Polynices. See Appendix 2.

Why not? I fathered you by sowing soil
where I was sown, without a question, blind.
     For you my tears are flowing, sightless tears,
imagining the bitter trials you'll face,
how you'll depend on others just to live.
What citizen assemblies will you join?
What festivals won't send you walking home   1490
in tears before you see the holy rites.
And when the season comes for you to wed,
my children, what's your prospect? Who will risk
the foul reproaches, damaging to all
the children I begot and all of theirs?
What evil's missing there? Your father struck
his father down and plowed the very field
where he was sown and thus acquired you
from that maternal soil that gave him birth.
Amid such mocking, who will marry you?   1500
The answer's simple: no one will. It's clear
you're doomed to die as maidens, barren earth.
     Now you, Menoeceus's son, alone
are left to be their father—since the two
of us who gave them life have perished. Please
don't let them wander, poor, unmarried kin,
or suffer hardships comparable to mine,
but pity them. Regard their tender age,
possessing nothing, save what you provide.
Touch me, my noble lord, and nod your head!   1510

     (Creon puts his hand on Oedipus' shoulder and nods
     his head.)

If only, children, you were old enough
to understand, I'd offer much advice.
As is, just pray for somewhere safe to live
and lives a little happier than mine.

CREON:
You've accomplished all you can by weeping.
        Go inside.

OEDIPUS:
Very well—although it's bitter.

CREON:
                    Timeliness is fair.

OEDIPUS:
Do you know my terms for leaving?

CREON:
                    Hearing them, I will.

OEDIPUS:
Make me live outside this land.

CREON:
                    That gift's the god's to give.

OEDIPUS:
I'm the one the gods detest!

CREON:
                    Perhaps you'll get your wish.

OEDIPUS:
Promise me!   1520

CREON:
        I'm not too fond of empty promises.

OEDIPUS:
Very well. Lead on.

CREON:
                    This way and let your daughters go.

OEDIPUS:
No! Don't take away my girls!

CREON:
                         Stop issuing commands!
Power's left your retinue. It wasn't yours for life.

(Exeunt Creon, Oedipus, and the others.)

CHORUS:
Native residents of Thebes, consider Oedipus,
one who solved the famous riddle, mightiest of men.
Everyone who looked on him was jealous of his fate.
What a flood of grim misfortune overwhelms him now!
Thus we learn how necessary seeing the final day
is for judging mortals blest. Otherwise refrain.
Happiness means ending life without being crushed by   1530
        pain.

Appendix 1.
The Riddle of the Sphinx

Although Oedipus and the chorus in *Oedipus Rex* refer to the riddle of the Sphinx, they never say what it was. Presumably it was well known in some form to Sophocles' audience, but, oddly enough, no version of it survives in classical literature. The earliest extant version is found in the *Deipnosophists* ("Wisemen Dining" 10.456b) by Athenaeus, a Greek scholar who flourished around 200 CE. His work is in the form of a wide-ranging conversation among learned dinner companions. It preserves hundreds of quotations from Greek literature and facts and fancies of every imaginable kind. Athenaeus quotes the riddle in the midst of a series of loosely related poems. He attributes his version to the poet Asclepiades of the third century BCE. It goes as follows:

> On earth there is a two-footed and four-footed creature,
>   whose voice is one.
> It is also three-footed. It alone changes its nature
>   of all the creatures
> Who move creeping along the earth, through the sky
>   or on the sea,
> But when it walks relying on the most feet,
> That is when the speed in its limbs is most feeble.

> (my translation)

The same version is found in other, later sources: the *Palatine Anthology* 14.64, the Scholia to Euripides' *Phoenissae* 50, and Tzetzes' commentary on Lycophron's *Alexandra* 7.

Appendix 2.
A Synopsis of Sophocles' Theban Trilogy

Oedipus Rex

Oedipus' parents were King Laius and Queen Jocasta of Thebes. Learning of an oracle that he would die at his son's hands, Laius ordered the baby Oedipus to be exposed on a mountain and drove a spike through his ankles. The servant entrusted with disposing of the baby was known only as Laius' man, a herdsman. Out of pity, he disregarded his orders and gave the baby to a Corinthian herdsman to pass on to foster parents. The Corinthian gave the baby to Corinth's childless royal couple, Polybus and Merope, who raised him as their own and named him Oedipus ("Swollen Foot") because of the spike's effects.

Years later a drunken comrade in Corinth accused Oedipus, now a young man, of being illegitimate. Distressed, Oedipus went to the Oracle of Delphi to ask who his real parents were. Instead of answering the question, the oracle told Oedipus that he was destined to lie with his mother, "producing a horrid brood," and to slay his father. Resolving to avoid that fate by never returning to Corinth, Oedipus fled from the oracle.

Coming to a crossroads, he turned toward Thebes. Here he encountered an elderly man with a group of servants. They quarreled over the right of way. When the old man swatted him with a goad, Oedipus threw him out of his chariot and killed him and all of his servants—or so he thought. In fact, there was one survivor: Laius' man. He ran back to Thebes with the story that a band of robbers had slaughtered King Laius and the rest of his attendants.

The citizens could not investigate the murder because a monster, the Sphinx, had appeared in the countryside, asking people a riddle and killing them when they failed to answer it correctly. At this juncture, Oedipus arrived in the city. Seeing him, Laius' man asked Jocasta for work in the countryside, far from town, and got his wish because he had always been a good servant. Oedipus confronted the Sphinx and answered her riddle, and she killed herself. The grateful citizens of Thebes made him their new king. He married the newly widowed queen, Jocasta.

Sophocles' play begins years later. Oedipus and Jocasta are the parents of grown children, two sons and two daughters. A plague is decimating the city. Oedipus' brother-in-law Creon goes to Delphi to learn why the gods are angry and is told that Laius' murderer must be punished.

Oedipus agrees to investigate the crime. He questions the old blind seer Tiresias, who suddenly remembers the truth, which he has been repressing. He says, "I knew these matters well, but I destroyed them. Otherwise, I hadn't come." Tiresias tries to refuse to talk. When Oedipus starts to badger him, Tiresias blurts out that Oedipus himself is the criminal whom he seeks. Oedipus' temper flares. He accuses Tiresias and Creon of using a fake oracle to overthrow him. Later Creon appears to defend himself, but Oedipus treats him scornfully too.

Jocasta emerges from the palace to soothe Oedipus. Learning that the quarrel concerns oracles, she belittles them, telling Oedipus that an oracle once predicted that her former husband would be killed by his son. Instead, she says, he was slain by a band of robbers . . . at a crossroads. Her reference to a crossroads disturbs Oedipus. He tells her about the journey that brought him from Corinth to a crossroads where he killed an old man who fit Laius' description. He sends for Laius' man, hoping that he will confirm his old story about a band of robbers.

While they wait for Laius' man, a Corinthian enters with news for Oedipus. His "father," Polybus, has died of old age, and the citizens of Corinth want to make Oedipus their king. Jocasta and Oedipus are relieved to hear of Polybus' death because it appears to invalidate the oracle predicting Oedipus would kill him. Oedipus tells the Corinthian that he cannot return because of the other part of the oracle: the prophecy that he would marry his mother. Thinking that this information will come as a relief, the Corinthian informs Oedipus that Polybus and Merope were not his real parents. He knows that Oedipus was adopted because the Corinthian is none other than the former shepherd who gave baby Oedipus to Polybus. He is, however, unable to tell Oedipus who his real parents are. Only a servant called "Laius' man" would know that. During these revelations, Jocasta leaves the stage.

Laius' man finally arrives. Oedipus demands to know who his parents are and threatens him with violence if he refuses to talk. Laius' man reluctantly tells him. Oedipus rushes into the palace, calling for a sword and demanding to see the queen. In an inner room, he finds that she has hanged herself. He removes brooches from her gown and jabs out his eyes. In a final appearance on stage, he says that he should now be sent into exile, although Creon tells him to stay in the palace for the time being. Oedipus exits with the help of his daughters.

Oedipus at Colonus

Homeless wanderers, the blind Oedipus and his daughter Antigone arrive in Athenian territory. Oedipus sits on a rock. When a local Athenian asks him to leave, since he is in an area sacred to the Furies, Oedipus replies that he must stay there. Then, learning that the king of the land is Theseus, he asks the Athenian to summon him. The Athenian says that he will summon other citizens to consider the request.

When the Athenian leaves, Oedipus tells Antigone about a prophecy that he must end his life in an area sacred to the Furies. He will be a blessing to those who receive him, a curse to those who drive him away.

A chorus of local Athenians arrives and persuades Oedipus to leave the sacred spot temporarily. They then press him to reveal his name. Since they have heard his story, they are horrified and want him to leave the region. When Oedipus and Antigone beg for compassion, however, the citizens agree to wait for the arrival of Theseus.

Oedipus' other daughter, Ismene, arrives on horseback. While Antigone has accompanied Oedipus on his wanderings, Ismene has brought him news from the city. Now she informs him that his sons, who originally planned to let Creon rule, are feuding over royal power. The younger, Eteocles, has seized power by winning popular favor. Driven into exile, the elder, Polynices, has married and made alliances in the region of Mycenae and hopes to conquer Thebes. Meanwhile, oracles speak of the importance of Oedipus in the imminent conflict. For this reason Creon is on his way to ask Oedipus to come back and live just across the Theban border—in order to honor the oracles without incurring pollution.

Oedipus recalls that when he first discovered the secret of his identity, he wanted to die. Then when he had calmed down and wished to live normally, he was driven out of the city, and his sons did nothing to help him, nor have they done anything for him subsequently. Only his daughters, he says, have acted like men. Oedipus is determined not to help either of his sons.

Members of the chorus say that libations must be poured to the Furies to placate them for Oedipus' violation of the grove. Ismene volunteers for the task. She is directed to the far side of the grove for water.

Theseus arrives and asks Oedipus what favor he seeks. It is to be buried in Athens, Oedipus says, and that city will benefit because his spirit will lead it to victory over Thebes if the two cities ever go to war. Because of this, Creon and his sons may try to seize Oedipus to prevent his burial in Athens. Theseus assures him that he will not allow that to happen.

After a choral interlude in which the site of the action is identified as Colonus, a suburb of Athens, Antigone announces that Creon is coming. Arriving, he declares that all the Theban people want Oedipus to return and that it is a shame for Antigone to lead such a wretched life. Oedipus refuses, emphasizing again that he was driven into exile when he wanted to stay in Thebes. Creon then reveals that his men have seized Ismene. Worse, he orders the seizure of Antigone. She is dragged offstage amid screams and wails.

Theseus returns to the stage. He orders the Athenian army to assemble to save the girls and scolds Creon for his illegal behavior. Creon says that he acted only because he did not think that Athens wanted to protect a man guilty of patricide and incest. This draws a furious rebuttal from Oedipus, who demands to know how he can be held responsible for crimes that were prophesied before he was even conceived. Laius, he says, was trying to kill him at the crossroads. If someone was trying to kill you, he asks Creon, would you defend yourself or would you ask him first whether he was your father? Theseus interrupts the diatribe to take action. He leaves with Creon to catch the Thebans who have the girls.

The chorus predicts that Theseus and his men will save the girls. As their song ends, Theseus delivers them back into Oedipus' arms. After they embrace, Theseus tells Oedipus that a man from the south has assumed a suppliant position at an altar of Poseidon and seeks to speak with him. Oedipus realizes that it is his son Polynices. He does not want to listen to him, but Theseus and Antigone persuade him to do so.

Polynices enters, bewailing his own misfortunes and those of Oedipus. He explains that Eteocles gained power in Thebes by winning over the people. In Argos, Polynices has raised an army with seven leaders, including himself. Oracles indicate that victory will belong to the side that Oedipus favors. If Polynices wins, he will restore Oedipus to Thebes. All he wants is Oedipus' forgiveness.

Oedipus replies that he is willing to talk to Polynices only as a favor to Theseus. Polynices and Eteocles are responsible for Oedipus' sorry condition. He curses them both, predicting that they will kill each other in battle.

Polynices' hopes are crushed. He asks Antigone to see that he is properly buried—if Oedipus' curse is fulfilled and she happens to be back in Thebes at the time. She begs him to give up his attack on the city, but Polynices says that would be cowardly. Antigone wants to know who will follow him after people hear about Oedipus' curse. He replies that as a good general he will conceal the truth. They part in tears.

Thunder sounds. It signals his death, Oedipus says, and calls for Theseus to return, so that he can lead Theseus alone to the secret place where Oedipus will die. Knowledge of this location and the other secrets Oedipus will tell him will keep Athens forever safe from attack by Thebes. The blind man leads Theseus and his daughters into the sacred grove. After a brief choral interlude, a messenger returns with the news that Oedipus is gone, having led the group to a basin where he bathed and said farewell to his daughters. "Everything that was me, has perished," he said. "You will no longer have the trouble of caring for me. I know how difficult it was, children, but one word alone dissolves all those troubles: love. The man does not exist who loved you more." After a tearful farewell, he sent them away.

When the group looked back from a distance, the messenger adds, Oedipus was gone, and Theseus stood shielding his eyes as though from some dreadful sight. "Either it was a messenger sent by the gods, or a power from below split the earth. He passed away without pain or disease, a marvelous end if ever a mortal's was."

The girls lament. Antigone asks Theseus to show her Oedipus' grave, but he refuses. The girls decide to return to Thebes to try to prevent their brothers from killing each other.

Antigone

Antigone confers with her sister, Ismene, outside the walls of Thebes. She asks whether Ismene has heard about the latest misfortune to befall their wretched family. Ismene knows only that their brothers have killed each other in battle and that the invading Argive army has fled. Antigone informs her that King Creon has issued a decree forbidding the burial of their brother Polynices because he was a rebel. The penalty for burying him is death by stoning. Will Ismene share in the work of burying him? Ismene replies that she cannot defy the law of the city. Antigone despises this attitude, saying that she would not accept her sister's help now even if she changed her mind and offered it.

Summoned by Creon, a chorus of leading citizens enters, singing of Thebes' glorious victory. Creon arrives and repeats his proclamation forbidding the burial of Polynices. The chorus says that they will support it.

A soldier enters, explaining at great length that he is extremely reluctant to make his report. He finally discloses that some dust has appeared on Polynices' body, and he was the unlucky soldier selected by lot to break the news to Creon. The chorus wonders whether the gods could have been responsible. Creon ridicules the idea, since Polynices intended to pillage their temples; rather, he thinks the guilty parties are people opposing him for financial reasons. He sends the guard back with stern orders to find out who sprinkled the dust. The guard is relieved to be getting away with his life. "There is no way," he tells Creon, "that you will see me coming here again."

The chorus sings an ode praising human inventiveness: "There are many amazing things, but nothing more amazing than man. He crosses the gray sea on the stormy blast," and more. The one problem for which man has found no solution is death.

The soldier appears on stage again, escorting Antigone and gleefully revealing that he himself caught her burying Polynices. He and his fellow soldiers had removed the dirt from the corpse and were guarding it carefully, sitting on the windy side to avoid the smell. At noon, there was a dust storm. When the sky cleared, Antigone stood over the body, wailing and pouring dust on it. She did not deny her guilt.

Creon asks Antigone whether she knew about his decree. She says that she did, but did not feel that it "enabled any mortal to violate the secure, unwritten laws of the gods; for they are not just for now and yesterday, but they live forever and no one knows their source."

Infuriated, Creon says that he would not be a man if Antigone overruled him. He decides that Ismene must have collaborated and orders her arrest. Brought before him, Ismene declares her guilt, but Antigone contemptuously denies it and insists that Ismene has no right to share in her death.

Ismene reminds Creon that his son, Haemon, is engaged to marry Antigone, but he is unmoved. "Other people," he says, "have fields fit to plow."

After a choral interlude, Haemon arrives. He begins very politely, saying that he respects Creon's judgment. Creon justifies his condemnation of Antigone with the argument that nothing is more important than obedience to authority. "It is necessary to protect authority," he says, "and never to be defeated by a woman. If one must fall, it is better to be beaten by a man. We would not wish to be called inferior to women."

Haemon suggests that Creon should consider the consensus in the city that it is unjust to execute Antigone. Creon replies that the people do not rule the city, he does, and he accuses Haemon of having been enslaved by a woman. Haemon in turn becomes angry and warns that if Antigone dies, she will destroy another. Creon interprets this as a threat against his own life. He orders Antigone to be brought to him so that she can be executed before Haemon's eyes. Declaring that *that* will never happen, Haemon storms out.

Creon orders the girls to be brought out for execution. The chorus asks whether he really intends to kill both. He instantly changes his mind: only Antigone must die, imprisoned in a rocky cavern with just enough food to allow her uncle to avoid guilt for murder.

Led to her prison, Antigone exchanges lamentations with the chorus. Creon repeats that it will be her choice whether to live or die in the cave. Antigone pauses to explain her devotion to her brother: a husband or a child could be replaced, but since her parents are dead, she will never have another brother.

After a short choral interlude, Tiresias enters, warning that the behavior of the birds and the appearance of the sacrificial meat show that the gods are angry over the mistreatment of

Polynices' corpse and the punishment of Antigone. Creon should reconsider.

At first Creon dismisses Tiresias, accusing him, like all prophets, of being interested only in money. Tiresias then makes a terrible prophecy. Creon will pay for the corpse that he denied to Hades with a corpse from his family, and cities will rise up against him.

Creon is shaken. After a brief exchange with the chorus, he heads out of town with servants to bury Polynices and free Antigone.

The chorus sings a song in honor of Dionysus, the Theban-born deity. At its conclusion, a messenger arrives with the news that Haemon is dead. This draws Eurydice, Creon's wife and Haemon's mother, out of the palace. She asks how his death came about.

The messenger was one of the servants following Creon. He reports that they first stopped to burn what remained of Polynices' corpse, then hurried to Antigone's cave. As they approached, they heard miserable groans, which Creon recognized as coming from Haemon. Inside the cave, they found that Antigone had hanged herself. Haemon was embracing her around the waist. Creon asked him to come out. Haemon glared at him with wild eyes, spat in his face, and lunged at him with his sword but missed. Then he plunged the sword into his own chest and fell on the girl, splattering her white cheek with his red blood.

At the end of the messenger's speech, members of the chorus notice that the queen has departed. The messenger goes inside to find out why.

Creon arrives carrying Haemon's corpse, cursing his previous blindness.

A messenger from the palace announces that Queen Eurydice has killed herself. The palace doors open to reveal her corpse. The messenger says that she stabbed herself in the stomach in front of an altar after cursing Creon for Haemon's death.

Creon asks to be led away, "as a foolish man who killed his son and wife without intending to." Contemplating all this, the chorus proclaims that wisdom is the most important ingredient in happiness.

Suggestions for Further Reading

Historical Background

Chadwick, John. *Linear B and Related Scripts*. Berkeley: University of California Press, 1987. The story of the discovery and decipherment of Mycenaean writing.

De Romilly, Jacqueline. *The Great Sophists in Periclean Athens*. Tr. Janet Lloyd. Oxford: Clarendon Press, 1992. A balanced assessment of the role of the sophists in Athenian culture.

Dickinson, Oliver. *The Aegean Bronze Age to Iron Age*. New York: Routledge, 2006. A survey of what is now known about the material conditions of Greece in the Dark Age.

Drews, Robert. *The Coming of the Greeks: Indo-European Conquests in the Aegean and the Near East*. Princeton, NJ: Princeton University Press, 1988. Analysis of the evidence for the date of the arrival of Greek-speaking Indo-Europeans in Greece.

———. *The End of the Bronze Age*. Princeton, NJ: Princeton University Press, 1993. An examination of explanations for the destruction of the Mycenaean palaces. After criticizing other views, the author defends the theory that changes in military technology and tactics made chariots obsolete and left palaces and cities at the mercy of piratical raiders.

Martin, Thomas R. *Ancient Greece from Prehistoric to Hellenistic Times*. New Haven, CT: Yale University Press, 1996. A brief, accessible survey of Greek history.

Murray, Oswyn. *Early Greece*. Atlantic Highlands, NJ: Human- ities Press, 1980. A detailed history of Archaic Greece from the end of the Dark Age to the Persian War.

Osborne, Robin. *Greece in the Making 1200–479 B.C.* 2nd ed. New York: Routledge, 2009. A history of Greece from the Mycenaean Age to the end of the Archaic Period. Distinguished by careful attention to the nature of the sources of our information and the way in which their statements about the past reflected their own circumstances and conflicts.

Pomeroy, Sarah B., Stanley M. Burstein, Walter Donlan, Jennifer Tolbert. *Ancient Greece: A Political, Social, and Cultural History*. Oxford: Oxford University Press, 1999. A history of Greece from Mycenae to the Hellenistic Age. Emphasis on social and cultural conditions as well as political and military ones.

Vermeule, Emily. *Greece in the Bronze Age*. Chicago: University of Chicago Press, 1964. The classic introduction to life in Mycenaean Greece.

Interpretations of *Oedipus Rex*

Ahl, Frederick. *Sophocles' Oedipus: Evidence and Self-Conviction*. Ithaca, NY: Cornell University Press, 1991. A defense of the surprising thesis that Oedipus was not the son of Laius and Jocasta and did not kill the former.

Berkowitz, Luci, and Theodore Brunner. *Sophocles, "Oedipus Tyrannus": A New Translation, Passages from Ancient Authors, Religion and Psychology: Some Studies, Criticism*. A Norton Critical Edition. New York: W. W. Norton, 1966. A prose translation and a selection of critical essays and other sources, including Thucydides' account of the plague in Athens.

Dodds, E. R. "On Misunderstanding the *Oedipus Rex.*" *Greece and Rome* 13 (1966): 37–49. A highly regarded essay arguing that Oedipus does not have a tragic flaw and that he is not the victim of fate. He is a hero who faces the fact that all human happiness is an illusion. Reprinted frequently (e.g., in Berkowitz and Brunner and in O'Brien).

Griffith, Drew. *The Theatre of Apollo: Divine Justice and Sophocles' Oedipus the King.* Montreal, Quebec: McGill-Queens University Press, 1996. Argues that Apollo brought about Oedipus' fall to punish him for his hubris.

Knox, Bernard. *Oedipus at Thebes.* New Haven, CT: Yale University Press, 1957. The classic presentation of the case that Oedipus may be understood as a symbol of Periclean Athens.

O'Brien, Michael. *Twentieth-Century Interpretations of Oedipus Rex.* Englewood Cliffs, NJ: Prentice Hall, 1968. An anthology of influential writings on the play.

Segal, Charles. *Oedipus Tyrannus: Tragic Heroism and the Limits of Knowledge.* Twayne Masterworks Series. New York: Twayne, 1993. Comprehensive background information and running commentary on the play for Greekless readers.

Vellacott, Philip. "The Guilt of Oedipus." *Greece and Rome* 11 (1964): 137–48. Defense of the interpretation that Oedipus knew that Laius and Jocasta were probably his real parents. Reprinted in Berkowitz and Brunner.

Ancient Greek Drama

Gregory, Justina, ed. *A Companion to Greek Tragedy.* Oxford: Blackwell, 2005. A collection of essays by leading scholars treating a wide range of topics related to Greek tragedy.

Rehm, Rush. *Greek Tragic Theatre.* London: Routledge, 1992. An engaging introduction, with attention to archaeological as well as literary evidence and interesting speculation about stage effects.

Storey, Ian, and Arlene Allan. *A Guide to Ancient Greek Drama: Blackwell Guides to Classical Literature.* Malden, MA: Blackwell, 2004. A good general introduction to Greek drama and some current scholarly debates.

The Delphic Oracle

Bowden, Hugh. *Classical Athens and the Delphic Oracle: Divination and Democracy.* Cambridge: Cambridge University Press, 2005. The influence of the Oracle of Delphi in Athens. A less skeptical consideration than Fontenrose's.

Fontenrose, Joseph. *The Delphic Oracle: Its Responses and Operations with a Catalogue of Responses.* Berkeley: University of California Press, 1978. A work debunking romantic conceptions of the oracle. Genuine oracles are said to have given straightforward approval of laws and religious decrees.

Mythology

Gantz, Timothy. *Early Greek Myth: A Guide to Literary and Artistic Sources.* Baltimore, MD: Johns Hopkins University Press, 1993. An exhaustive study of myths and legends, including that of Oedipus, as found in Archaic literary and artistic sources.

Sophocles' Life and Works

Lefkowitz, Mary. *The Lives of the Greek Poets.* Baltimore, MD: Johns Hopkins University Press, 1981. A deconstruction of ancient biographical writing, arguing that "facts" in ancient biographies are invalid inferences from fictional events in the authors' poems. Includes a translation with commentary of the ancient Life of Sophocles.

Scodel, Ruth. *Sophocles.* Boston: Twayne, 1984. A concise summary of what is known about Sophocles and a play-by-play analysis of his work by an excellent scholar.

The Tragic Flaw

Halliwell, Stephen. *The Poetics of Aristotle: Translation and Commentary.* Chapel Hill: University of North Carolina Press, 1987. A translation of and commentary on Aristotle's *Poetics* containing a balanced, up-to-date discussion of the *hamartia* controversy and other issues raised by Aristotle's essay.

Wisconsin Studies in Classics

General Editors

**William Aylward and
Patricia A. Rosenmeyer**

E. A. Thompson
Romans and Barbarians: The Decline of the Western Empire

H. I. Marrou
A History of Education in Antiquity
Histoire de l'Education dans l'Antiquité,
     translated by **George Lamb**

Jennifer Tolbert Roberts
Accountability in Athenian Government

Erika Simon
Festivals of Attica: An Archaeological Commentary

Warren G. Moon, editor
Ancient Greek Art and Iconography

G. Michael Woloch
Roman Cities: Les villes romaines by **Pierre Grimal,**
     translated and edited by **G. Michael Woloch,**
     together with A Descriptive Catalogue of Roman Cities by
     G. Michael Woloch

Rudolf Blum
Hans H. Wellisch, translator
*Kallimachos: The Alexandrian Library and the Origins of
    Bibliography*

David Castriota
Myth, Ethos, and Actuality: Official Art in Fifth Century B.C. Athens

Barbara Hughes Fowler, editor and translator
Archaic Greek Poetry: An Anthology

John H. Oakley and Rebecca H. Sinos
The Wedding in Ancient Athens

Richard Daniel De Puma and Jocelyn Penny Small, editors
Murlo and the Etruscans: Art and Society in Ancient Etruria

Judith Lynn Sebesta and Larissa Bonfante, editors
The World of Roman Costume

Jennifer Larson
Greek Heroine Cults

Warren G. Moon, editor
Polykleitos, the Doryphoros, and Tradition

Paul Plass
*The Game of Death in Ancient Rome: Arena Sport and
    Political Suicide*

Margaret S. Drower
Flinders Petrie: A Life in Archaeology

Susan B. Matheson
Polygnotos and Vase Painting in Classical Athens

Jenifer Neils, editor
Worshipping Athena: Panathenaia and Parthenon

Sinclair Bell and Helen Nagy, editors
New Perspectives on Etruria and Early Rome

Barbara Pavlock
The Image of the Poet in Ovid's Metamorphoses

Paul Cartledge and Fiona Rose Greenland, editors
Responses to Oliver Stone's Alexander: *Film, History, and
    Cultural Studies*

Amalia Avramidou
*The Codrus Painter: Iconography and Reception of Athenian Vases
    in the Age of Pericles*

Shane Butler
*The Matter of the Page: Essays in Search of Ancient and
    Medieval Authors*

Allison Glazebrook and Madeleine Henry, editors
Greek Prostitutes in the Ancient Mediterranean, 800 BCE–200 CE

Norman Austin
Sophocles' "Philoctetes" and the Great Soul Robbery

Sophocles
A verse translation by David Mulroy, with introduction and notes
Oedipus Rex